Joseph Pickford of Derby

St Helen's House, Derby

Joseph Pickford of Derby

Edward Saunders

ALAN SUTTON

First published in the United Kingdom in 1993 by
Alan Sutton Publishing Ltd
Phoenix Mill · Far Thrupp · Stroud · Gloucestershire

First Published in the United States of America in 1993 by
Alan Sutton Publishing Inc. · 83 Washington Street · Dover · NH 03820

British Library Cataloguing in Publication Data

Saunders, Edward
  Joseph Pickford of Derby
  I. Title
  720.92

  ISBN 0-7509-0380-5

Library of Congress Cataloging in Publication Data applied for

Jacket erratum: for Caulke Abbey please read Calke Abbey.

Typeset in 11/13pt Baskerville.
Typesetting and origination by
Alan Sutton Publishing Limited.
Printed in Great Britain by
Redwood Books, Trowbridge, Wiltshire.

Contents

For Howard Colvin
who first introduced me
to Joseph Pickford and made
this modest volume possible.

Foreword
by the Duchess of Devonshire

I welcome this book on Joseph Pickford for several reasons; one of them is very personal. He was the architect of a building I pass, and admire, almost every day of my life, the old Grapes Hotel which is now the Chatsworth Estate Office and Club at the entrance to the park. The pleasure of looking at this delightful example of Pickford's work of 1776 is enhanced by the fact that it is built of redbrick, which makes a welcome change to the eye from the stone houses in the village of Edensor.

The 5th Duke of Devonshire commissioned Pickford to build an hotel where the sightseers visiting Chatsworth (already open to the public) could put up. It replaced the 'wretched inn, noisy and disgustful' which, until then, had been the only available lodging.

His rectory at Edensor, alas, is no more, but the county of Derbyshire can still show many examples of the work of Joseph Pickford in the unmistakable style of the latter half of the eighteenth century, so much admired today.

Through this book we can learn about the man and his buildings, thus adding greatly to the architectural knowledge of those of us who are lucky enough to live in the county and the countless thousands of people who come every year to admire its beauties, both natural and man-made.

Debo Devonshire

Author's Preface

It might be of interest to the reader to know how I first became acquainted with the work of Joseph Pickford. After leaving school in 1950 I was articled to Samuel Morrison, architect of Derby, and, as part of my studies as a probationer of the Royal Institute of British Architects, was required to make a measured drawing of a building of architectural merit.

Even at the age of nineteen I had an interest in the eighteenth century and chose for my subject 44 Friar Gate in Derby, which the authorities assured me was the work of Robert Adam. It was, they said, built by Adam, together with 41 Friar Gate, at the same time as Kedleston. At least they had the date right, and I had no reason to doubt their judgement.

Shortly afterwards, when cycling through Ashbourne, I noticed a house in the Compton which was identical to No. 44, except that it was built in stone. Even then I did not doubt my superiors, though I began to wonder how Adam, with his workload, found so much time for small local commissions.

After the completion of my articles I moved to T.H. Thorpe and Partners, who had their offices in 41 Friar Gate, now the Pickford House Museum. Again in Ashbourne, I noticed the great similarity between No. 41, and the façade of the Mansion, which, as a student of James Boswell, I knew to be the home of Johnson's friend Dr John Taylor. About this time I became friendly with Helen Boswell, a direct descendant of the Boswell's of Auchinleck. Her grandfather, a medical practitioner, had his surgery in the Grey House in Church Street, opposite the Mansion. It was by a very curious coincidence that Boswell had dined there in 1777 with the owner, Brian Hodgson. All of these houses I was later to discover were the work of Joseph Pickford.

My interest in architectural history was cut short by my National Service, and I did not take up the study again until the 1970s, when I first became acquainted with Howard Colvin's *Dictionary of English Architects*. It would not be fanciful to say that this volume revolutionized my whole approach to the subject. I realized for the first time that it is not possible to write about architecture without the facts, which Colvin supplied in abundance. Through him I first learned that an architect named Joseph Pickford had built a house of some pretension in Derby Friar Gate. Without this knowledge this book could not have been written and is the main reason why I have chosen to dedicate it to him.

The form of any book is largely dictated by the information available, which, alas, in this case is not over abundant. As no Pickford archive survives, I have had to rely on parish registers, occasional letters, accounts and the like, which provide little more than the dry facts. We know next to nothing about the man himself. Something of his character can be deduced from what his clients say about him, but as these comments come mainly from one source, Josiah Wedgwood, and are largely derogatory, they must be treated with care. Clearly there was another side to his character, as we know he had the ability to make and keep friends like Joseph Wright, the painter, but any opinions of good report have long since disappeared.

I have divided the book therefore into two parts. Part one is a brief biography, and account of Pickford's working practice, followed by a detailed description in part two of his individual works. From time to time no doubt more facts will come to light, and if any readers do come across such information I would be most grateful if they could pass it on to me.

I would like to thank the people who have given me the most help and encouragement: Howard Colvin, who read the script with great patience and suggested numerous improvements; Maxwell Craven, whose knowledge of Derby and Pickford's friends is second to none. It is probable that without their help this book would never have been completed.

I would also like to give a sincere vote of thanks to my friend Ivor Shaw for his excellent photographs and unstinted devotion to his craft. Not for him the quick snap. No general planned his strategy with greater care, or waited with such patience for the sun to come out, or some idle delivery person to remove his vehicle.

Finally I would like to remember my friend Penny Lee, whose culinary skills greatly eased the tedium of the long hours of drudgery involved in compiling this book.

Edward Saunders
Ticknall, Derbyshire
1993

PART ONE:

JOSEPH PICKFORD
1734–82

CHAPTER ONE

Family Background, Childhood and Apprenticeship

On 7 September 1694 the town of Warwick was devastated by a fire that reduced the greater part of St Mary's church to rubble and left many of the citizens homeless. According to the inscription on the newly built tower, it was a 'conflagratione stupenda', but what was an ill wind for the townspeople served the building trades very well. Although the fire in Warwick in no way compared with the Great Fire of London, the same conditions prevailed and the opportunities for building brought in ambitious men with new ideas.

Of these, the most prominent were Francis Smith (1672–1738), and his brother William (1661–1724) who came from The Wergs, near Tettenhall in Staffordshire. They were the sons of a bricklayer and were brought up in the building trade, William as a bricklayer like his father and Francis as a mason.[1] In 1697 they were contracted to rebuild the nave and tower of St Mary's church, to the designs of Sir William Wilson,[2] after which Francis settled in the town to become 'Smith of Warwick', the most respected master builder in the Midlands with a large country-house practice in the neighbouring counties.

Some of the craftsmen Smith needed for his work lived in Warwick, others came in from outside. Among these were the Pickfords, a family of masons skilled in supervision as well as in working stone. There were at least six brothers: William, Joseph, Thomas, Richard, John, and James, and two sisters, Elizabeth and Sarah.

As the Pickford family are first recorded in Shropshire it is probable that they hailed from that county. William Pickford, the architect's grandfather, was occasionally called Pitchford, a Shropshire village which took its name from a natural bituminous well in the vicinity. This William and his wife Constance settled in the village of Badger in that county shortly before the baptism of their first recorded child, William, the architect's father, on 26 October 1673,[3] but they were not natives of that place as the family name is not recorded in the Hearth Tax Returns for the previous year, 1672.[4] Why William chose to put down his roots in Badger is not clear, but between 1673 and 1687 five of

St Mary's church, Warwick

their children were baptized in the village church after which their name disappears from the parish register.

It is possible that William Pickford was working on a nearby house like Patshull, but with a growing family chose to leave his wife behind when he moved on in search of new work. It is not known where the sons trained, but as Tettenhall, the base for the Smith family, is only ten miles from Badger, and we next encounter the younger William Pickford living in Warwickshire close to Francis Smith's first large country-house commission, it is not unreasonable to suppose that they had known each other since childhood.

This dearth of information is not surprising as the life of a mason in the eighteenth century was still akin to that of a vagrant. Necessity ensured he was constantly on the move seeking fresh employment; the pay was poor and by no means guaranteed; illness and a bad winter when work was stopped brought many to the verge of starvation. Conditions were bad enough for the skilled craftsman, but for the labourer, earning a shilling a day, they were intolerable.

To counter these uncertainties families banded together to help each other and those who achieved success assisted the less fortunate. Fatherless boys were taken on as apprentices and girls were bequeathed dowries to assist them in their quest for husbands, which more often than not they found among their brothers' friends. Working tools, drawing instruments, books of architecture and even articles of clothing were passed from generation to generation as family heirlooms. The Pickford family were no exception and fitted this description exactly.

It is not known to whom or where the younger William Pickford was apprenticed, but it was probably in Warwickshire, for as soon as he had completed his indentures he was contracted to marry a girl from that county. The licence, dated 28 October 1694, reads:

> William Pickford of Tanworth in the County of Warwick, aged 21, and a bachelor, intends to marry Rachel Wincote of the same, aged 21, and a maiden, to be married in the parish church of St Nicholas, in the borough of Warwick.[5]

Of further interest is the hitherto unknown first marriage of Francis Smith a few months later in the same village. The licence on this occasion, dated 30 January 1695, reads:

> Which day appeared personally Francis Smith of the parish of Tetnal (Tettenhall) in the County of Stafford, aged 24, and a bachelor, and attested that he intended to marry Mary Morteboys of the parish of Wotton Wawen in the County of Warwick, aged 22 and a maiden . . . and prayed licence to be married in parish church of Tanworth. . .[6]

Tanworth church, Tanworth in Arden, Warwickshire

The marriage took place next day on 31 January 1695.

Andrew Archer of Umberslade was the patron of the living of Tanworth which seems to confirm Howard Colvin's suggestion that Francis Smith was responsible for building Umberslade Hall, *c.* 1695–1700, the first of many country-house commissions. There are no contemporary building records for the house, but a Warwickshire historian writing in 1815,[7] said that Umberslade was built by 'John Smith', who is also referred to elsewhere in the book as the builder of 'St Mary's, Warwick'. It would appear that he had the right builder, but gave him the wrong Christian name.

Umberslade is a plain, nine-bay, stone-fronted house, and not a very distinguished design, but well within the compass of the 24-year-old Francis

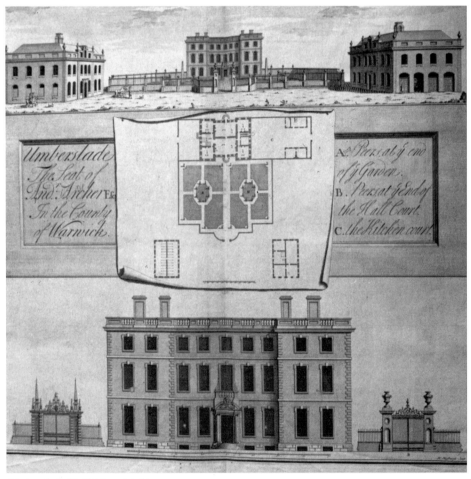

Umberslade Hall, Warwickshire

Smith, no doubt assisted by an even younger William Pickford. As Andrew Archer was the brother of the architect Thomas Archer, it is difficult to understand why he did not consult him about the design. A possible explanation could be that at this date he had not turned his attention to architecture, as his first recorded commission was for the Duke of Devonshire in 1704.[8]

The marriage of Francis Smith to Mary Morteboys did not survive the first year, as Mary was dead by December 1695 when her baby daughter Elizabeth was baptized in St Mary's church, Warwick.[9] Presumably she died in childbirth, but there is no record to confirm this. Thereafter Francis made Warwick his home and in 1702 married a local girl, Anne Lea, who was to be the mother of William Smith the younger (1705–47), who succeeded to his father's practice after the latter's death in 1738.

William Pickford and his wife Rachel settled in Tanworth, though presumably this was only a convenient base for his work, which eventually took him to most of the midland counties in the employ of Francis Smith. The parish records show they had at least four children, William, John, Elizabeth and Mary, which leads to confusion, because after the death of Rachel in 1730 William married again, and had a second family including the architect, Joseph Pickford. As the children of the first marriage are not mentioned in William Pickford's will of 1742 it must be assumed that they were either dead or well established and not needing their father's help, probably the former.

William Pickford was the eldest of the six brothers and seemed to be the dominant member of the family as he later drew at least two of his younger brothers to Warwick in search of work. The most successful was Thomas Pickford (1681–1748) who became a leading mason contractor in the town, but it now appears that he was preceded by his brother Richard, who was baptized at Badger in April 1676. His marriage licence, dated 2 September 1700, declares that

> Richard Pickford of the parish of Badger in the county of Shropshire, aged 24, and a bachelor, intends to marry Elizabeth Silk of the parish of the Blessed Virgin, in the Borough of Warwick, aged 22, and a virgin.[11]

By this date the new tower of St Mary's church was half built, an enterprise which seemed to owe not a little to the skills of the Pickford brothers.

The other two boys baptized at Badger; Joseph in March 1684, and James in June 1687, were still apprentices when the tower was finished in 1704, but it is reasonable to suppose that they also began their careers in Warwick. Joseph moved to London where he became one of the leading sculptors and mason contractors of his day. James is an enigma. He too may have moved to London and if he did the James Pickford working for Sir William Chambers in the 1760s was probably his son.[12]

The earliest reference to a member of the Pickford family working for Francis Smith occurs in the accounts for building the stable block at Croome Court, Worcestershire, in 1719. This reads:

> 1719 April gave Mr Smith ye builder 63 3 0.
> Gave then his Stone Mason Pixford 10 6.[13]

As no Christian name is given we cannot know for certain which Pickford this was, and the same applies to the 'Mr Pickford' who was working for Francis Smith at Melbourne, Derbyshire, in 1727. He is described 'as an experienced man' and was responsible for making the drawing of Thomas Coke's gate house, 'done according to your Hon'rs draft' which is still in the muniment room at Melbourne today.[14]

There is no record of a Pickford with a Christian name until after the death of Francis Smith, when in April 1738 William Pickford witnessed a receipt for money paid to William Smith the younger, for the 'New Building' at Trentham in Staffordshire.[15] Four years later in 1742 a 'Mr Pickford' was supervising the construction of Catton Hall, Derbyshire, again for William Smith.[16] It is possible that this was William Pickford, but as he died in July of that year it is more likely to have been one of his brothers.

Rachel Pickford died in 1730 when her husband was fifty-seven years old. Fifty-seven then was considered to be late middle age, but this was no bar to William who remarried almost immediately and began a new family. As yet we do not know where this marriage took place, only that the second Mrs Pickford was named Mary, and that William settled her in the tiny village of Ashow five miles north of Warwick. There can be no doubt that this William, and the husband of Rachel Pickford are one and the same, as signatures on Pickford's will and the papers relating to the administration of Rachel's estate are identical.[17]

Ashow is still a most attractive hamlet of redbrick and timber-framed houses in the water meadows by the River Avon, but there is no obvious employment there for a mason unless he was connected with the building of Stoneleigh which stands close by. The Pickfords are not recorded in the Stoneleigh accounts of this date, but Thomas worked there after William's death. In 1743 he was responsible for building the dog kennels to the designs of William Smith the younger. Lord Leigh kept a large pack of hounds and the payment of £298 to Pickford for the masonry suggests it was no ordinary kennel, but a building of some architectural pretension.[18]

William and his wife Mary had four children, all boys, baptized at Ashow. John on 12 March 1732, Joseph on 6 October 1734, Thomas on 13 February 1737 and William on 6 January 1742.[19] This corrects one misunderstanding. At his death in July 1782, the *Derby Mercury* gave Pickford's age as forty-five, we now know he was forty-seven, three months

Ashow church, Ashow, Warwickshire

short of his forty-eighth birthday, that is assuming he was baptized immediately after his birth.

William Pickford died in July 1742, five weeks after his infant son, William. He was then sixty-eight years old and apparently still working, as the will called upon his brother Thomas to assist his wife in valuing his stock.

It would be difficult to imagine a more desirable resting place than the churchyard at Ashow. From the south door of the church, the ground falls away to the banks of the River Avon. In the space between a number of early gravestones survive, all dating from the time of the Pickford brothers, but the harsh winter weather has long since erased the inscriptions and it is no longer possible to say which, if any, marks William Pickford's final resting place.

The will[20] gives a little information about William's background. All of his property in Warwick he bequeaths to his wife Mary during her natural life, after which he divides it between his five surviving children: Elizabeth, Mary, John, Joseph and Thomas. This consisted of three houses on Wilson's Hill, and other property in Saltsford. Recognizing that his family had to be educated he gives Mary the power to mortgage or sell the property in Saltsford, 'for the support, maintenance and education of my said wife and children during their minority.' Finally, he appoints his wife as his executrix and bequeaths to her the residue of the estate.

After her husband's death Mary Pickford continued to live at Ashow with her family. She may have received assistance from her brother-in-law, Thomas, as he was more than generous to her children after his own death in July 1748. He was either a bachelor or widower, we are not told which, but clearly he had no children of his own.

In his will[21] he describes himself as 'Thomas Pickford of the Borough of Warwick, mason.' To his nephews Joseph and Thomas he bequeaths £135 each, a bond of the Corporation of Warwick for £100, all his linen, his two best pairs of breeches and six of his best books. To his brother Joseph he bequeaths £50 to take care of his nephews and put them out as apprentices to good trades. He does not specify a particular trade, but as he bequeaths his working tools 'to Ralph Salt and my nephew, Joseph', clearly he intended the boy to be a mason.

We do know a little about Ralph Salt, Joseph's uncle by marriage, as he married Sarah Pickford in Lichfield Cathedral in October 1742. He too was a mason, and possibly came from Ellastone in Staffordshire, where a family called Salt with a preference for the Christian name Ralph flourished in the eighteenth century.

Apart from the children of his brother William, Thomas also remembers his own brothers, sisters and brother-in-law. They receive small sums of wearing apparel like his brother, Richard, who was the recipient of his 'wiggs and best hat'. Finally as his executor, he appoints his 'loving friend, George Eborall', a member of a family as distinguished in the joiners trade, as the Pickford's were masons.

As William's eldest boy John does not appear in the will it must be assumed he was dead. The two girls both married at Ashow: Mary to John Timm in January 1748, and Elizabeth to Thomas Judd in April 1752. Apparently they were not local men as their names do not appear again in the parish records. Thomas, Joseph's younger brother, stayed close to home. He married young, and with his wife, Hannah, had three children baptized at Ashow. It seems they were satisfied with their lot, as their descendants were still living in the village in the late nineteenth century.

Some time in the autumn of 1748, young Joseph, now fourteen years old, left Ashow to take up an apprenticeship with his Uncle Joseph in London. For an orphan his prospects were good. He had money of his own, but more than that his uncle was one of the leading architectural craftsmen in the country and well able to guide his nephew towards his chosen profession.

What little we know about Joseph Pickford senior, (1684–1760) suggests that he was a man of outstanding ability. After leaving Badger he began his career as an assistant to the Italian sculptor Giovanni Battista Guelphi, who in 1715 was working on the restoration of the Arundel Marbles for Lord Pomfret.[22] Vertue tells us that Guelphi was brought to England by Lord Burlington who employed him for many years in London and at his villa at Chiswick. It is likely Pickford worked there too, because later he found most of his employment among the group of architects associated with Lord Burlington.

If this was so, Pickford must have had a tactful nature as Guelphi was not an easy man to work for. Vertue, who clearly had no love for him, says he was 'a man slow of speech, much opinionated and as an Italian thought nobody could be equal to himself in skill in this country.' As a final dig he adds, 'It is thought Lord Burlington parted with him very willingly.'[23]

In December 1734, the year Guelphi left England, Pickford married Mary Atkinson at St Bride's church in Fleet Street. They were both of mature years; she was a widow with a grown son, he was a bachelor or widower already fifty years of age. Pickford in his will describes his partner, William Atkinson, as his son-in-law. We suppose by this he means stepson, as there is no record to show he had a daughter. When young Joseph joined his uncle, the family consisted of Pickford, his wife and her son, with probably an apprentice or two living in.

The move from Ashow to the hurly-burly of the capital must have caused young Joseph a little disquiet, but he was quick to learn the ways of the cosmopolitan world. Certainly in later life he was no man's fool. By any standard he was a shrewd businessman, well able to see through the machinations of dishonest tradesmen, something he was accused of being himself. Many years later Josiah Wedgwood consulted him about setting up a showroom in Great Newport Street. Wedgwood wrote to his agent: 'Mr Pickford . . . says we are likely to be imposed upon. He is a Londoner and knows all their tricks.'[24]

The house in which Joseph Pickford senior lived and carried on his business stood at the top end of Piccadilly, between Brick Street and Down Street, a site now occupied by the Park Lane Hotel. Horwood's map of 1795 shows the house as one of a row facing on to Green Park. With a rateable value of £24 it was larger than its immediate neighbours, but still comparatively modest in size.[25] The map does not show any access to the rear, but this probably passed through the building to the yard behind, which contained both the workshop and the stable.

At the beginning of the eighteenth century there were many such builders' yards and forges in what is today the heart of Mayfair. The reason was that the locality lay outside the jurisdiction of the Worshipful Companies of the City of London. The Masons' Company and others still had the power to control building in the City. Where they could they regulated apprentices and extracted dues from their members, which, rightly or wrongly, was resented by the freer spirits in the West End.

The names of the great craftsmen who worked in the vicinity are recorded in the rate books. They were of all trades, but the blacksmiths included Jean Tijou, Jean Montigny, and Thomas Robinson. To these must be added the sculptors and masons: John Nost, Andrew Carpenter, John Cheere and of course Pickford.[26]

By the time Joseph joined his uncle most of these people had either moved on or passed away, but the tradition of fine workmanship still survived. Pickford, through his excellent connections, enjoyed the confidence of the leading architects of the day, in particular William Kent who gave him constant employment. He worked for Lady Isabella Finch at her house in Berkeley Square, thought by some to be Kent's masterpiece[27] and afterwards for many years at Holkham Hall in Norfolk.[28] His final contract for Kent was the masonry for Henry Pelham's house in Arlington Street. The architect died before the building was finished, but Stephen Wright, Kent's assistant, took the work over and formed an association with the builder that was to continue until Pickford's death.[29] The bond between them was such that Pickford named Wright as one of his executors.

During the years of Joseph's apprenticeship his uncle was employed on two of the finest Palladian buildings in England: the Horse Guards in Whitehall[30] and the University Library at Cambridge.[31]

The Horse Guards was designed by Kent, but was not begun until three years after his death, when his designs were realized by his followers, John Vardy and Thomas Robinson. The building minutes show Andrews Jelf and Joseph Pickford were the principal masonry contractors. In August 1751 Jelf was working on the central block and Pickford on the Horse Guards wing. Young Joseph was then nearly seventeen years old.

Joseph Pickford senior was not a Patent Artisan appointed by the Board of

Engraving of the Horse Guards, Whitehall, London

Works, nor, as far as we know, had he been employed in any capacity on the Royal Works before this date. It would appear that his name had been attached to the list of approved craftsmen at the insistence of Henry Pelham (1695–1754) whose house in Arlington Street he had recently completed. Pelham, as Chancellor of the Exchequer, was a powerful man, and but for his death in 1754 he would no doubt have put further work Pickford's way. As it was this task fell to his brother, Thomas Pelham-Holles, Duke of Newcastle (1693–1768). It is said that Thomas had a genuine affection for his younger brother, and judging from their correspondence this would seem to be true.[32]

The Duke of Newcastle, as Chancellor of the University of Cambridge, was in an excellent position to insist upon his choice of both architect and builder for the new University Library at Cambridge, which was erected in the years 1754–58, to the designs of Stephen Wright. The elegant, arcaded façade that stands at right angles to the Senate House is the finest Palladian building in Cambridge and excellent model for any aspiring architect to study. Pickford and Atkinson were paid nearly £5,000 for their work, but it was Atkinson who seems to have done most of the carving, including four large heads, representing the seasons, vases and festoons of fruit and flowers.

These two buildings and Holkham Hall, where Joseph Pickford senior worked for many years, were all designed by architects influenced by Lord Burlington (1694–1753), the driving force behind the English neo-Palladian

The University Library, Cambridge

Movement in the eighteenth century. For Burlington this meant a return to the architecture of antiquity as explained and illustrated by Andrea Palladio in his *Four Books of Architecture*, published in Italy in 1570. The English translation by Isaac Ware, published in 1738, was the copy most readily available and the one which the young Joseph Pickford almost certainly studied. But Burlington's puritanical urge to preach absolute classical standards was not a path many chose to follow. Lesser mortals, like Pickford, governed more by fashion than intellect, spiced their designs with rococo embellishments. This is not to denigrate their work, but only to say that the deviations they made from the principles of Palladio would not have met with the approval of Lord Burlington.

It is easy to point to the buildings which influenced Pickford, but we still do not know where or when he studied architecture. Many masons practised as architects, but he was clearly trained as one. He was a fine draughtsman who understood the art of chiaroscuro and could lay a watered ink wash to perfection. Because of his uncle's close association with Stephen Wright, it is possible he had some formal training in an architect's office, or failing that, at an institution like Shipley's Drawing Academy in St Martin's Lane. One thing is certain, his London training gave him a head start over his rivals in the provinces, both as a craftsman and as an architect.

Apart from his studies in architecture and antique drawing, Pickford's education was all of the practical kind. His handwriting, like his draughtsmanship, was very stylish, but he wrote as he must have spoken, in a midland dialect. This is not to disparage his learning, but only to suggest he never attended a grammar school or studied Latin. Like many tradesmen he had enough education to draw up accounts and write fawning letters to gentlemen clients, but he probably never read a book that was not directly connected to architecture. When the Italian architect Gianantonio Selva visited Pickford in Derby, he expressed surprise that such an accomplished architect had never visited Italy. But this was really a tribute to those who taught him the fundamentals of classical design, which showed the depth of understanding that was commonplace in England.

What little we know about the family at Hyde Park Corner is contained in the will of Joseph Pickford senior drawn up in June 1751,[34] some nine years before his death. The principal legatees were his wife, Mary, his stepson and partner, William Atkinson and his nephew, Joseph Pickford, described as 'the eldest son of my brother, William'. As executors he appointed William Atkinson and the architect, Stephen Wright.

Pickford died in 1760 (the exact date is not known), aged seventy-six. His death was certainly not expected, as he was not buried at his parish church, St George's, Hanover Square, so it is possible he died in the country while away on business. The will was proved in December 1760 and the administration granted to Atkinson.

For some reason Stephen Wright refused to serve. Why this was so is not explained, but it is just possible that young Joseph Pickford was at the root of the problem. Twenty-five years later the Duke of Newcastle was still employing Stephen Wright, but not the Pickford family. In 1775 Wright was building Clumber Park in Nottinghamshire for the duke, but preferred to have the chimney pieces carved at enormous expense in London than favour his old friend's nephew a few miles away in Derby. It was not as if local tradesmen were ignored. Benjamin Yates of Derby, the ironsmith, wrought the balustrade to the gallery, and more importantly, John Whitehurst, Pickford's friend, was consulted about the design of the waterclosets. According to his account Whitehurst made 'sundry visits' from Derby to Clumber and it would have been extraordinary if Pickford had not been mentioned in his conversations with Wright.

Whatever the disagreement between the beneficiaries of Pickford's will, Stephen Wright had no wish to be part of it. The outcome being that twenty years after the testator's death his wishes had still not been carried out. By this time everyone involved, except Joseph Pickford, was dead. He took out fresh letters of administration and presumably inherited what remained of the estate.

Briefly, Pickford's principal assets after his wife and stepson had shared his stock in trade and the money owed by the creditors, were three houses and the yard by Hyde Park Corner. The income from these he left to his wife during her natural life, then to his stepson and finally to Pickford. After his wife's death the rents from the two side properties were to be divided between Pickford's two sisters, Elizabeth Bradley and Sarah Salt, during their natural lives. Finally, the share of the capital arising from the business which had gone to Mary Pickford was to be divided after her death 'between the families of my brothers and sisters and their children'. It was this last clause which probably led to the disagreement.

Considering the amount of money which must have passed through Pickford's hands, and judging by the standards of successful contractors, he was not a rich man. Andrews Jelf, with whom he shared the contract for building the Horse Guards, left a country house, a flourishing business, considerable London property, and over £30,000, when he died in 1759.[35] It is useless to speculate why Pickford was not more successful, though it is true that the masons who accumulated the greatest wealth were often quarry owners as well, suggesting that more money was to be made out of extracting stone than working it.

The date of Mary Pickford's death is not known, but it is possible she predeceased her husband, as the payment of the rates on the family house and yard was taken up immediately after Pickford's death by Atkinson in the spring of 1760. Thereafter, he continued to live in the house until his own death in

1766. In 1762 Atkinson married, which further complicated the problem, as after Atkinson's death the property reverted to Pickford. They must have reached a mutual agreement as the widow, Sarah Atkinson, continued to live there until 1772.

The problem with the will was that it set the interests of the Pickford family against those of Mary Pickford and her son. It is easy to imagine the discontent in far away Warwickshire if the rents on the side cottages did not arrive on time. And yet, who can blame Atkinson if he dragged his feet, for what were these people to him? It could not have been the intention of Pickford to knowingly poison the atmosphere in this way, and certainly if his wife had predeceased him it is surprising he did not draw up a new will.

Young Joseph probably left London to return to the Midlands before his uncle's death, as we know that in the autumn of 1759 he was working in Derbyshire. It seems there was no place for him in his uncle's firm, but this is only supposition. Perhaps he had decided independently to make his life in the Midlands and left without regret. Certainly he was an ambitious man and if he had wished to stay in London the small matter of a will and a hostile environment would not have deterred him. As it was he chose to return to the place where he was born and build himself a practice among his own people.

CHAPTER TWO

The Architect

When Joseph Pickford came of age in October 1755 he was probably still living with his Uncle Joseph by Hyde Park Corner, but there is no record of his movements in the next three years. In the building trade it was usual for an apprentice to serve his master for seven years and after the completion of his indentures to seek employment as a journeyman. In Pickford's case this may not have been so, as he clearly had greater skills and expectations than the average apprentice mason. In fact it is doubtful if he ever 'worked on the tools' as they say in the building trade, for his first known appointment in the summer of 1759 was supervising the workmen at Foremark Hall in Derbyshire, a house designed by David Hiorne of Warwick, one of his father's old associates.[1]

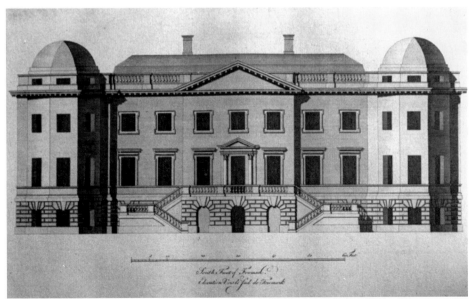

Foremark Hall, Derbyshire

After the death of William Smith the younger in 1747, William Hiorne and his brother David became principal master builders in Warwick and largely succeeded to the Smith family practice in the midland counties. David Hiorne, who is credited with the design of Foremark, died in 1758, the year before the building was started.[2] Although his authorship is not doubted, it does seem that Pickford, who worked at Foremark for over a year as site architect, did make some contribution to the final design.

As far as we know Pickford had no connections in Derbyshire other than those which his father might have made while working for Francis Smith. But these, backed by a lively personality and a will to succeed, were clearly enough. In 1760, shortly after the completion of Foremark, Pickford took lodgings in Derby in order to exploit these new found contracts. His principal patron at this time and his best hope for advancement seems to have been Wenman Coke, a nephew of the Earl of Leicester who lived at Longford Hall, a Tudor mansion eight miles west of Derby.

Coke was the son of Lady Anne Coke, the earl's sister, and Major Philip Roberts of the Horse Guards. In 1750, as Wenman Roberts, he inherited Longford from his uncle, Edward Coke, and assumed the family surname and arms. But this was only a prelude to a greater prize, as it was suspected he would also inherit the great estates of the Earl of Leicester. For this he had to wait until after the earl's death in 1759 when Holkham among other choice plums passed to him. The celebrations that followed included a portrait by Reynolds of Wenman Coke's five-year-old heir posing as the 'Young Hannibal' and a face-lift for Longford Hall, Pickford's first recorded architectural commission.

Joseph Pickford senior worked at Holkham for many years and was well known to Wenman Coke's Derbyshire agent, Thomas Wilkins, the father of Pickford's future bride. In the early 1750s Pickford senior rode up to Derbyshire to select alabaster for lining the hall at Holkham.[3] At Longford he met Wilkins who conducted the negotiations and together they rode over to the quarry at Fauld in Staffordshire. We know Pickford stayed one night at the Dog and Partridge in Tutbury and probably at Longford as well. It was possibly through this contact that the younger Joseph Pickford obtained an introduction to his chief patron and his wife's family, which almost certainly persuaded him to make Derbyshire his home.

Mary Wilkins seems to have been an excellent match for Pickford, but all we know about the marriage are the bare facts taken from the licence. The wedding took place at Longford church in April 1762. We are told that the groom was a mason, aged twenty-six, and a bachelor of the parish of St Peter's, Derby. The bride was aged twenty-two, the daughter of Thomas Wilkins and a spinster of the parish of Longford in the county of Derby. This is yet another variation on Pickford's age, for if the register at Ashow is correct he was at least twenty-seven, seven months short of his twenty-eighth birthday.

Nothing is known of Mary's early life, but clearly she had the managerial skills of her father, as after her husband's death she ran a worsted mill, first with a partner, but later on her own account. There is no known portrait to record her appearance nor anecdote to illuminate her character, yet we know she was a woman with a distinct personality of her own. She and her husband were two of a kind, sturdy and independent, determined to make their own way in life, come what may.

An architect, or any professional man, in Georgian England needed to be young, healthy and blessed with superior talent, because the reward for failure was all too often ignominy and the debtors' prison. No doubt it was possible even then to succeed without help, but what every young architect dreamed of was a patron who gave employment, or better still, introductions to his friends.

For some years the gentlemen in Derbyshire, headed by the Duke of Devonshire, had been dithering over the building of a new County Assembly Rooms. In 1763 a design was produced by an amateur architect, Earl Ferrers, of Staunton Harold, and a subscription list opened. Possibly through the good offices of Wenman Coke, Pickford was given the job of executive architect, responsible for organizing the labour and supervising the erection of the fine building which was to grace the Derby Market Place for the next two hundred years.[4]

The Derby Assembly
Rooms, Derby

Though he was still a young man he had already gathered around him the nucleus of workmen who were to be his chief support in the years ahead. He himself spoke with some pride of his 'very good sober masons', and in the account book for the Derby Assembly Rooms we learn their names for the first time. Very few of them were Derby men, for the most part they had followed Pickford up from Warwickshire to work at Foremark and then decided to continue in his employment. The best known are the Eglington brothers. Like Pickford they were men of ambition and several of them later made good on their own account.

It was about this time that Pickford first became acquainted with the group of midland intellectuals associated with the Lunar Society, in particular, Joseph Wright, the painter (1734–97), Peter Perez Burdett, the cartographer and engraver (1735–93)[5], and John Whitehurst, the clockmaker and geologist (1713–88).[6] Not that Pickford was noted for his interest in scientific matters, but it was through them, and Whitehurst in particular, that he met a number of his most important clients.

Thomas Mozley, writing in the nineteenth century about his own early life, devotes a whole chapter in his *Reminiscences* to the architect's younger son, the Reverend Joseph Pickford. Although he has nothing good to say about him, he does give some interesting facts about the father, most of which can be verified. Mozley begins:

> There are men who are interesting from their associations, but whom no associations can redeem. Such was Joseph Pickford. I first became acquainted with his figure and circumstances at Derby in 1815. His father had been an architect and builder and an intimate friend of Wright, the painter . . . and also of Whitehurst, a mechanician and author of the *Theory of the Earth*. It was a coterie contemporaneous and on friendly terms with the Philosophical Society founded by Erasmus Darwin, but with a difference of caste, for philosophers are socially as exclusive as other people.[7]

The most obvious proof of this association was the portrait Wright painted of the Pickford children.[8] When Mozley called on the Reverend Pickford it was still in the house. He continues:

> The only pretty thing in his sitting room was a charming picture, by Wright, of Pickford and his brother playing with a spaniel, of the date of 1785, I should think, and in the gay costume of that period.

But malicious as ever he concluded: 'When I called on Pickford it was a caution to see what a beautiful child might come to.'

The Pickford children by Joseph Wright

The portrait of the Pickford children appears in Wright's account book as 'A conversation piece of two of Mr Pickford's children £63'. It dates from the years 1776–7, when Joseph, the younger of the two sitters, was four years old, and his brother Thomas, seven. The painting depicts the two children cuddling their dog in a classical landscape. The background is conventional, but the garden temple seen through the trees may have been an allusion to their father's profession.

As no reference to Pickford is to be found in Wright's account book, it is assumed he never painted the architect's portrait. Yet this is by no means certain as Wright frequently portrayed his friends without charge. In this category of work, Wright's biographer, Benedict Nicolson, illustrates a portrait he calls 'a young artist'.[9] The portrait, dating from the years 1769–70, shows a calm, self-assured, young man of about thirty, holding in his hands what Nicolson calls 'a draughtsman's tool', but which to us looks like an architect's ruling pen. Nicolson continues:

> We can guess from the nervous tension of cuffs and shirt ruffle and by the sympathy expended on the face that he is a personal friend [in Derby? Lichfield? Liverpool?] . . . it would be surprising if this young man did not turn out to be someone who figures in these pages.

'The Young Artist' by Joseph Wright

The portrait today is part of a Derbyshire collection where it has been since the original owner or his family disposed of it. This alone should have suggested to Nicolson that the sitter was a local man. We cannot ascribe this portrait with certainty, but Pickford seems to be the most likely candidate. In 1769 Pickford was thirty-five, the approximate age of the figure in the portrait. In that year he was building his house in Derby, a usual occasion for a portrait to be painted. There the matter must rest until the painting is cleaned and the background, now obscured with dirt, revealed.

It is possible that Pickford and Wright first met in London not Derby. Wright spent two periods of study under the London artist, Thomas Hudson, in 1751–3 and 1756–7, but he was also in the capital regularly thereafter.[10] Pickford seems to have been well known to the architect Sir William Chambers, or at least to two of his pupils, James Gandon (1743–1823) and Edward Stevens (1744–75), both of whom were friends of Joseph Wright.[11]

James Gandon, according to his son, made Wright's acquaintance in the 1760s as fellow members of the Howdalian Society. This was a club for young artists designed to bring together professionals practising music, art and architecture, curiously named after a Captain Howdall of the Royal Artillery. John Hamilton Mortimer was the president and they met weekly at Munday's Coffee House in Maiden Lane. 'On these occasions Mr Wright was an efficient member, possessing an agreeable voice and a perfect knowledge of music.' Gandon often spoke of 'the many pleasant hours he experienced as member of that society'.[12]

The County Hall, Nottingham

We are not told if Pickford was a member, but he was well known to James Gandon. In 1770 Pickford built the Nottingham County Hall to Gandon's designs,[13] and further proof of their association came when Gandon included Pickford's Sandon Hall as well as Foremark in the volume of *Vitruvius Britannicus* which he published in 1771.[14] Edward Stevens was another pupil of Chambers known to both Pickford and Wright. Stevens' principal architectural commission was Doveridge Hall, Derbyshire, which he designed for Sir Henry Cavendish in 1769.[15] In October 1770 Thomas Mottershaw of Derby promised to carry a message to Pickford from Josiah Wedgwood. He later wrote to say he was unable to call at Doveridge and could not pass on the message, which seems to indicate that Pickford was the contractor building the house.[16]

In 1774 Stevens went to Italy to study, but was taken ill almost immediately and died in Rome in June 1775.[17] Wright himself went to Italy in 1774 and made contact with him. In July 1775 he wrote from Parma to Ozias Humphrey in Florence speaking of 'poor Mr Stevens', so presumably he had already heard of his death.[18] That Wright was on familiar terms with architects and was interested in their work cannot be doubted, as on his return from Rome he brought in his luggage an architectural drawing associated with a design Clerisseau had made for the Empress of Russia.[19]

The second of Pickford's close Derby friends, John Whitehurst, was born in Congleton in 1713, but lived in Derby from 1737 to 1775.[20] His house and works in Queen Street, originally a seventeenth-century building with a hipped roof and a lantern, was refronted with a unified façade in 1764. No contemporary illustrations of the house exist, though an early photograph shows the upper storeys shortly before demolition. The combination of Venetian and Diocletian windows with stone dressings in a brick façade are typical of Pickford's early work and there can be little doubt that he was the architect.[21]

Though Whitehurst had little formal education he was a man with great natural talent in both the mechanical arts and philosophical speculation. In the view of his friend Erasmus Darwin, 'his integrity and humanity were rarely equalled in any station of life'. He gained his reputation as a clock and instrument maker, though all branches of mechanics and natural philosophy were one to him. He himself took greatest pride in his treatise, *An Enquiry into the Original State and Formation of the Earth*, published in 1778.

Some time after May 1765 Whitehurst and his scientific friends in the midland counties, including Matthew Boulton and Erasmus Darwin, started to hold informal meetings to discuss their mutual interests thus founding the Lunar Society. But it was not until the mid-70s that the name 'Lunar' first appears, and regular meetings were not held until 1780. These meetings were usually held at Matthew Boulton's house in Birmingham, where the members dined together each month on the night nearest to the full moon.[23]

John Whitehurst by Joseph Wright

John Whitehurst's house, Queen Street, Derby, in the late nineteenth century

Engraving of John Whitehurst's house in Queen Street, Derby

The founder members were quickly joined by others, including James Watt, Thomas Day, Richard Lovell Edgeworth, Samuel Galton, James Keir, Joseph Priestley, and Josiah Wedgwood. As a society for scientific discussion it was without equal in Europe and no fewer than eleven of the fourteen members became Fellows of the Royal Society. Whitehurst acted as a catalyst for the other members and it now appears he made important suggestions to Watt which enabled him to perfect his steam engine.[24]

In 1775 Whitehurst was appointed Stamper of the Money Weights on the recommendation of the Duke of Newcastle.[25] In that year he was advising the Duke on plumbing matters at Clumber Park which may have led to the appointment.[26] Thereafter he quit Derby and moved to London where he spent the rest of his life in philosophical pursuits. His house in Bolt Court, Fleet Street, became a meeting place for men of science of every nation and rank.[27]

As early as December 1760 Pickford wrote to Matthew Boulton to offer his services as an architect. In his letter her refers to a meeting in Birmingham and in a postscript sends his duty to Dr Ash who was later a frequent guest at the Lunar Society meetings and friendly with all the members including

Whitehurst. Nothing seems to have come from Pickford's appeal, but in 1774 he secured the commission for building St Mary's church in Birmingham and Dr Ash was a leading member of the building committee.[29]

In 1767 Whitehurst introduced Pickford to another member of the Lunar Society with unfortunate results. Josiah Wedgwood was looking for an architect builder for his new house and works at Etruria in Staffordshire and selected Pickford on Whitehurst's recommendation. The job started well, but soon sank into the realms of farce with Pickford chiefly to blame.

Wedgwood's meticulous correspondence tells us a lot about the pitfalls that awaited the unwary client in the eighteenth century. The pity is that we see their relationship only from Wedgwood's point of view; Pickford is damned as a rogue and though he deserved censure Wedgwood was not an easy man to work for. Pickford's best defence lay in the quality of his product. Though Wedgwood had nothing good to say of his architect, his house was received with acclaim.[30]

Another friend of Pickford and Wright was Peter Perez Burdett who was born in 1735 at Eastwood, Essex, the son of William Burdett who had married the daughter and heiress of the Reverend Peter Perez, the vicar of that place.[31] He may have received his training as a surveyor during a period in the army, but by 1760 he was living in Derby making surveys of gentlemen's estates

P.P. Burdett and his first wife Hannah, by Joseph Wright

under the patronage of Earl Ferrers, and for a time lived at Staunton Harold.[32] Shortly afterwards he married an older, and possibly richer, wife, and began work on his celebrated map of Derbyshire which was published in 1767.

In 1765 Burdett and his wife were painted by Wright in a landscape that appears to be Knowle Hill, a secondary estate of the Burdett family about three miles from Foremark.[33] It would seem that by posing in such a location Burdett was trying to establish his credentials as a cadet branch of the family, but it did him little good as he was always in a scrape for money however much his friends tried to assist him. Perhaps it is significant that John Whitehurst had begun to make surveying instruments about this time and probably gave Burdett the introduction to Wedgwood that led to their experiments with aquatinting on pottery, yet another of Burdett's ideas which came to nothing.

We know that Wright and Earl Ferrers lent Burdett money, probably to build his house in All Saints' churchyard, a rococo Gothic edifice which was ready for occupation by 1768. In that year Burdett, pursued by creditors, left the town to seek a better fortune in Liverpool where Wright joined him some months later.[34] We believe Pickford was the architect of Burdett's house, but the only evidence we have of him working in the Gothic style is the fine drawing he made for a new window in St Mary's church, Nottingham.

At this distance in time it is not always easy to put a finger on the common link that joins a particular group of friends, but in the case of Wright and Burdett, and possibly Pickford as well, it was love of music. Both Wright and Burdett were known to be excellent musicians, and in Derby they had many opportunities to practice their skills.

Musical life in the town centred around William Denby, the organist at All Saints' church, who was appointed in 1743, two years before the first modern organ was installed there. It was at his home in the 1760s that Derby's musical élite performed in concert for their own pleasure and that of their friends. We know that these virtuosi included William Denby's son, Charles, and the Reverend Mr Blackwall, the curate of St Peter's, on violins, Burdett on cello, Wright on flute, and the Reverend Charles Hope on harpsichord continuo.[35]

It is not known when Pickford's claims as an architect were first brought to the attention of the Duke of Devonshire, but this again was probably the work of John Whitehurst. Another of his scientific friends was the Reverend John Wood, the rector of Edensor and chaplain to the duke. The Wood family seat, Swanwick Hall, built around 1772, bears the imprint of the Derby architect, but Edensor rectory, which we know he designed for Wood in 1776, stood by the gates in Chatsworth Park until it was demolished in the nineteenth century. From this came a number of commissions from the duke including the Edensor Inn and the Devonshire Hospital in Derby.

P.P. Burdett's house in All Saints' churchyard, Derby

Wood's connections are very interesting. After ordination in 1749 his first appointment was as curate to the Reverend William Mason, at Aston near Rotherham. Mason was a friend of the poet Gray and tutor to Lord George Cavendish, the younger brother of the duke.[36] Through Mason, Wood became acquainted with Edward Delaval, the electrical experimenter, John Whitehurst, Erasmus Darwin and Anthony Tissington, the geologist and mining engineer, who lived at Swanwick and was already known to the Woods.

Another friend in their group was Benjamin Franklin. Delaval and Franklin were members of the committee set up in 1769 to report on a suitable means of securing St Paul's Cathedral against lightning. Franklin visited Whitehurst on several occasions in Derby and continued to correspond with him after the war with the American colonies began, which accords with all we know about the political sympathies of Devonshire and his circle.

Through his contact with Wood, Pickford became part of the political web which controlled the county and borough of Derby in the duke's interest. As Tennyson wrote of another great magnate, he was truly 'the master of half a servile shire', though in fairness to the duke it must be said that he was a generous patron to the town, though not everyone saw him in this light.

The Edensor Inn, Chatsworth, Derbyshire

Parliamentary elections presented the duke with difficulties because there were enough independent burgesses in the town to make the outcome uncertain. This problem was overcome by creating a sufficient number of honorary burgesses, known as 'faggots', or in Derby, 'Peak Burgesses'; usually tenants or such who owed their interest to the duke. One such levy took place in April and June 1776, when over one hundred burgesses were admitted in three weeks. Against this outrage, 'A Real Burgess' published a broadsheet listing what he called 'these servile sycophants', a list headed by the name 'Joseph Pickford of Derby, builder'.[37]

'A Real Burgess' had much to be indignant about, for he tells us:

> While every member of that noble family is bellowing for the liberties of America and boasting of their Revolutionary Tenets, they are jointly sapping the Constitution here, in open defiance of those patriotic principles they occasionally profess.

Just so, and for good measure he adds:

> It might be asked when they strenuously opposed American Taxation without Representation, they recollected that to secure seats for members of his family, the Town of Derby was deprived of the freedom of election by a large number of honorary burgesses.

Shortly afterwards Pickford was co-opted as a member of the Derby Corporation in the Whig interest.[38]

When we talk of Whigs and Tories it is important not to confuse the politics of the eighteenth century with those of the present time. Modern political systems are based on the balance of power between capital and labour reflecting the nature of our industrial society. England in Pickford's day was not industrial, nor was the working class enfranchised.

We cannot presume that Pickford had no interest in religion or the affairs of state, but clearly like all tradesmen his first concern was turning an honest penny. His lot was that of a lackey in the service of a great duke, which makes it all the more remarkable that he also enjoyed the patronage of Lord Scarsdale at Kedleston, the rival centre for political power in Derbyshire. It says a lot for Pickford's tact and competence when his predecessor, James Denstone, was dismissed because his Whiggish sympathies upset his lordship.[39]

Another group to which Pickford belonged was the Freemasons. Their claim to be above politics may in part explain the wide range of opinions to be found among his clients. The secrecy with which they surround their lodges and their curious rituals lead many people to poke fun at them, or worse, detest them root and branch, but their eighteenth-century records are very comprehensive, and they freely opened their archives for this study.

The thought that Pickford may have been a Mason was first suggested when it was discovered that John Whitehurst stamped the Masonic device of the square and compass on the inside of some of his clock movements.[40] He is listed in later life as being a member of the London Lodge of Emulation No. 21, but there are no records of his initiation. Joseph Pickford, or at least *a* Joseph Pickford, is listed as a member of a lodge that met at the Three Compasses, Silver Street, Golden Square. Pickford was a Londoner so it is only natural that he should have belonged to a London lodge. As James Gandon was also a Mason it seemed at first sight that the Howdalian Society may have been a lodge, especially as it was named after a captain in the artillery, but if it was, it is not recorded.

Other friends and clients of Pickford are listed as members including Lord Ferrers, the Duke of Devonshire, William FitzHerbert of Tissington, and Josiah Wedgwood. It is possible that Wedgwood took to Pickford on their first meeting because of their common interest in Freemasonry. If this was so, it was a liking that did not survive, or in any way sweeten, their business relationship.[41]

It is perhaps unfortunate that Pickford was also involved in the failure of Heath's Bank in Derby, the greatest business scandal suffered by the town in the eighteenth century. To describe John, Isaac and Christopher Heath as hard businessmen would be an understatement; they were unscrupulous rogues. Their speciality was buying up mortgages, foreclosing and selling the properties over the owners' heads. In this they seem to have been associated with Pickford, as his name was frequently linked with theirs in disposing of foreclosed property.[42]

The Heath's banking house is still standing at the entrance to Lock-Up Yard in the Cornmarket in Derby. Apparently they leased the premises from the Bateman family.[43] Pickford was the architect, but it is not known whether he built it for the Batemans or the Heaths. The building is now in multiple occupancy and little of the original interior has survived, but the façade facing the Cornmarket is more or less intact and stands out against the other buildings in the street, including what remains of the Duke of Devonshire's town house next door.

In most of their unpleasant activities the Heaths had the law behind them, but in March 1779 they overstepped the mark and were themselves declared bankrupt.[44] Mary Ann Denby recounted the story in a letter to her brother, William. She was the sister of Charles Denby, the friend of Joseph Wright.

Our town is filled with moanings and complaints by the failure of Messrs John and Christopher Heath, bankers, who have involved the whole town

Christopher Heath by Joseph Wright

and country in ruin . . . Their proceedings have been most unjust . . . I will give you a specimen or two. They let the Holdens have a lease of Darley Hall for their lives in consequence of which they expended £2000 on it. Well Sir, since this affair it has come out that they mortgaged this very place to Boldro (Boldero) and Co., great bankers in London . . . before they had granted the lease. I look upon such people as no better than highwaymen, for if the Holdens purchase they must pay for their improvements (twice over) . . . Every day we hear of something fresh. Poor people that have had their all in his hands . . . and poor Simpson, the dancing master, put £200 into their hands, but a week before they stop't. There are thousands more sufferers.[45]

Darley Hall, Darley Abbey, Derbyshire

To this sorry tale it is only necessary to add that Pickford was responsible for the alterations to Darley Hall, and we now know that Holden's lease from Heath included a proviso that any work done to the house should be undertaken by Pickford.[46] It is possible he was an innocent party and knew nothing of the machinations of the Heath brothers, but in view of his close involvement with their business dealings it is doubtful if the victims of the fraud took such a charitable view. As always it was those who could least afford it that suffered. The poor dancing master had the spring taken out of his heels, but the perpetrators of his misery escaped scot-free. With what he inveigled out of the bankruptcy, Christopher Heath settled in Duffield where he lived to the age of ninety-six and died in July 1815, 'much respected'.[47] As Mr Peachum says in the *Beggar's Opera*, 'There is no spot nor stain that money can't remove.'

It is a pity that most of the evidence we have concerning Pickford's affairs suggests that he was unscrupulous in his business methods, but there was clearly more to him than that. It is very doubtful if he would have retained the confidence of a man with the integrity of John Whitehurst unless there was another side to his character.

Over the years Pickford expended a lot of effort building up his architectural reputation and, but for his premature death, would have established himself as a leading figure in his profession. As it was the major commission eluded him. There is no reason to suppose that the Duke of Devonshire was dissatisfied with his work, but it was John Carr of York who built the Crescent at Buxton, a commission that might well have gone to Pickford had he lived.

A major outlet for architectural talent in the eighteenth century was speculative building, but Derby was not Bath and there was no call for the squares and terraces which gave men like John Wood the chance to show off their skills in town planning. The development of Friar Gate after 1768 was the nearest equivalent. In this Pickford played a leading part, but the houses were individual dwellings and lacked the impact of a unified design.

The finest building in Friar Gate is Pickford's own house. According to Thomas Mozley people said it was his 'chef d'oeuvre', but there is reason to suppose the architect thought otherwise.[48] When he was visited by Gianantonio Selva in 1781, it was St Helen's House in Derby that Pickford took him to see.[49] There seems little doubt that this ashlar-faced Palladian mansion built in the grand style was more to his liking and nearest to his heart.

At no time in his life did Pickford advertise in newspapers like ordinary builders, which suggests that most of his work came through introductions from satisfied clients. This is not surprising as in provincial terms he was a first class architect. He brought to his designs a sophistication which all too often

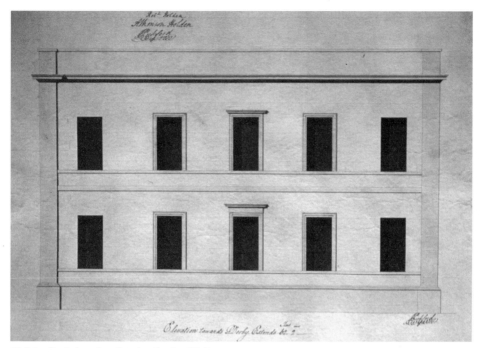

Pickford's design drawing for Darley Hall

was lacking in his competitors. The minor country seats he designed are easy to recognize because of their excellent style and proportions. None more so than Darley Abbey, the house he remodelled for the unfortunate Holdens. The late Sir Nikolaus Pevsner had never heard of Pickford, yet he was clearly taken with his work at Darley Abbey. Of the façade facing the park he wrote, 'Simply late Georgian, uncommonly well-proportioned with widely spaced windows.'[50]

Joseph Pickford died on 13 July 1782 at the age of forty-seven. By modern standards he was still a young man with many years of his working life ahead of him, but for him it was not to be. The *Derby Mercury* printed a short formal obituary:

> On Saturday night died age 45 [*sic*] after a short illness at his house on Nun's Green, Mr Joseph Pickford, an eminent builder and one of the brethren of this corporation. He was a tender husband, a kind father and much respected by all his friends and acquaintances.[51]

He was buried in the parish church of St Werburgh, a short walk from his home in Friar Gate. Apparently his burial took place inside the church as a payment was made to the churchwardens for taking up the floor. There is no monument to mark the place, but that is not surprising as most of the nave was demolished when the church was extended in the nineteenth century. With his death the business was wound up and the stock sold at public auction.[52] The family now had sufficient money to live as gentlefolk and no doubt were at pains to forget how their wealth had been created.

Pickford seems to have been very fortunate in his choice of a wife, for what we know about Mary Pickford suggests she was a spirited, independent woman, well capable of managing her own affairs. She appears briefly in the diary of William Bagshaw Stevens, the headmaster of Repton School, as the woman who introduced him to the Derby Rout. He speaks of 'Beau wits and giggling belles . . . with noise and nonsense clattering round the board'. Clearly the house in Friar Gate was once a very happy place. We catch an occasional glimpse of her in Pickford's letters to Francis Russell, the London agent to the Duchy of Lancaster. Once she sent Russell a salmon, and on another occasion took a letter by hand to London, confirming her independent way of life. She lived to a good age and was buried next to her husband in St Werburgh's church in April 1812.

Which brings us to the two sons. The eldest Thomas, named after Pickford's brother, died in June 1790, aged twenty-one, after a 'lingering illness', leaving only Joseph. For his life we have two sources: one hostile, Thomas Mozley and one friendly, William Bagshaw Stevens.

Mozley, who first made Pickford's acquaintance in Derby in 1815, has nothing good to say of him. He saw him as a pathetic creature, defective in character and countenance. 'As long as I remember,' he wrote, 'Pickford had an angry eye and carbunculous complexion', and much else in a similar vein. At Oriel College, Pickford was the 'active, tidy and clever little builder's son from Derby', which is the best he could say of him.

The anecdotes he recounts are all against Pickford and none are very funny. 'When he mounted his pulpit at his small Derbyshire living, he took out his account book instead of his sermon, and was a long time fumbling at it without finding his mistake', is typical of what he has to offer. In short Mozley was a pompous humbug totally lacking in sympathy for those he thought intellectually inferior to himself.

Not everyone was so scathing about the Reverend Joseph Pickford; William Bagshaw Stevens saw him in a very different light. To Stevens he was 'Lucky Pickford', because of his election to a Fellowship of Oriel College, Oxford, at the age of twenty-one.

In July 1792 'the Pickfords', mother and son, took their holidays at 'Black Pool', the nearest seaside resort to Derby, some three days' ride away, at that time noted for good lodgings and bracing air. There they met Stevens with a party of his friends *en route* to the Lake District. Though only nineteen years old, young Joseph took the fancy of the ladies, in particular Kitty Arden, who was considered a great beauty. After such an auspicious start in life it is difficult to understand how he became the cantankerous bore Mozley claimed to know.

According to Mozley, Reverend Joseph Pickford never married, though he gave the impression at Cholderton, his living in Wiltshire, that he had a wife and family to support in Derby. He was friendless, save 'for two respectable young women from Nottingham' who visited him from time to time. It is not known if he intended them to benefit from his estate, but if Mozley is to be believed, at his death in March 1844 the 'seven or eight thousand he had scraped together', passed to the 'keeper of an apple stall in Warwick'.

As always the truth is more prosaic. Pickford's heir was in fact one William Pickford, described as a 'yeoman of Trafalgar Road, Greenwich'. Nothing is known about him, though he was probably a spendthrift, as he mortgaged the house in Friar Gate to Thomas Evans of Darley Abbey who successfully foreclosed in 1850. This final indignity marked the end of the Pickford family connection with the town of Derby.

CHAPTER THREE

Architectural and Building Practices

The architect as we know him today is a product of the Renaissance and was unknown in England before Inigo Jones turned his attention to architectural design in the early seventeenth century. Because architecture does not rank as a liberal art and was not studied at universities, the design of buildings prior to this date was largely left to the building tradesmen themselves. The masons and carpenters who built the medieval cathedrals were also responsible for the designs. That some of them, like Henry Yevele, were men of genius cannot be denied, but they were not architects in the modern sense. That is, a professional man set apart from the building trades by education and specialized training, his skills acquired by academic instruction rather than by practical experience.

Another significant difference centred around the overall control of the building process. In a medieval building each trade was responsible for all the work pertaining to their own craft; thus the mason designed the stonework and the carpenter the roof. Westminster Hall, one of the greatest medieval buildings in England, was the result of a happy combination of the genius of Yevele the mason, and Hugh Herland the carpenter, and it says a lot for Yevele's restraint that he did not attempt to detract from the magnificence of Herland's roof. While this method worked well when the design was arrived at by an empirical process after much discussion, it would not do for an architect who conceived his building as a whole, basing his design on a complicated system of mathematical proportions. At this point the tradesman was left behind and the architect assumed complete control.

When Pickford was a young man the architectural profession, such as it was, was still in a fluid state. It had no proper organization, the Royal Institute of British Architects was not granted its charter until 1834, and outside of London it was virtually impossible to study architecture, or architectural draughtsmanship, as an art form.

This lack of an academy was in part made good by the Office of Works. The most famous architects of the day sat on the Board, and it was through the agency of the King's Works that so many skilled master craftsmen became acquainted with the latest ideas in design and decoration. By 1730 Lord Burlington (1694–1753), the Yorkshire amateur architect with a passion for the works of Andrea Palladio, had gained control of the Office of Works and aided by his followers had imposed Palladian formulae upon the public buildings of London.

This architectural hold, which amounted almost to a tyranny, was reinforced by publications like Campbell's *Vitruvius Britannicus*, published by subscription in three volumes in 1715, 1717 and 1725, and Isaac Ware's translation of Palladio's *Four Books of Architecture* in 1738. These and other publications by like-minded disciples of the Italian architect spread the word throughout the country and established a style of architecture in public buildings which survived until the present century.

In this scheme of things Joseph Pickford was still akin to the medieval mason. Although he considered himself to be an architect, he was clearly not a person of independent means who studied architecture as a dilettante. For Pickford, architecture was always an optional extra. The bulk of his living he made from building, and he never pretended otherwise.

To understand how Pickford organized his building business it is necessary to take a closer look at one of his projects. We are fortunate in that at least one of his specifications and estimates has survived. This is a scheme for rebuilding part of Keele Hall in Staffordshire for Ralph Sneyd in 1761 at the very outset of his career. The drawings which accompanied the specification have disappeared, but this does not affect our understanding of his working methods.[1]

What Pickford called an estimate was a fixed price sum to construct the building in accordance with the drawings and detailed specification. In this he undertook to supply all of the labour and materials, except what he could salvage from the old building and reuse. His masons were to obtain the stone for facing the building from the quarry on Sneyd's estate.

In the eighteenth century there were no building contractors as we know them today. By which we mean a single company prepared to undertake the entire building operation with its own employees supervised by competent foremen. Thomas Cubitt (1788–1855), though trained as a joiner, is now acknowledged to be the first general contractor in the modern sense of the word.

The method Pickford practiced, with many other mason contractors of his day, was to tender a figure for the entire operation, but to sublet the work of the other tradesmen, retaining only the masonry for himself. This system was largely forced upon him through lack of capital. No one at that time had sufficient resources to keep armies of tradesmen on the payroll. If it was not possible in London it was certainly beyond the means of a provincial builder.

It was not until after the Napoleonic Wars, when contracts greatly increased in size, that men like Cubitt were able to build up sufficient resources to stay in business beyond the life-span of one man so that the business gained a momentum of its own. But even he had to resort to speculative development to keep his men fully employed.[2]

The problems which arose from Pickford's method of working came about largely through lack of control; both over the workmen, who were not employed directly, and over the quality of the building materials. These problems could be overcome by keeping a competent clerk of works on the site, but this was not always possible, and on at least one occasion dishonest workmen combined with their supervisor to defraud Pickford who was left to settle matters with an unsympathetic client. Problems of this kind are difficult to control even with modern methods of communication, but when the next county was a day's ride away, it was almost impossible.

To return to Keele Hall, nine months after submitting his estimate, and sensing that his price was too high, Pickford wrote again to Sneyd offering to do the work on a different basis:

> But still Sir I can't say I can give so just account as if everything was new, and not repairs, therefore had much rather find the workmen and give you the exact account of everything and as to my trouble leave it intirely to you. But I may venter to undertake it for the above sum if your Hono'r had much rather the work was done by estimate.

The problem with this method was that Pickford had no incentive to keep the cost down as he had when working for a fixed sum. The workmen, too, were on a fixed daily rate and if the mood took them could stretch the job out to the crack of doom. Fortunately for Sneyd he declined his offer, but in 1763 Pickford undertook to build the Derby Assembly Rooms by this method with disastrous results.

If this suggests that building tradesmen led a pampered life nothing could be further from the truth. In a letter to Ralph Sneyd, Pickford speaks of his 'good honest sober masons',[3] but they were only his in the sense that they had attached themselves to him as the most likely source of employment. They had no prospects of pay until Pickford had first extracted the money from his employer. Men like Josiah Wedgwood knew this and deliberately withheld payment, confident that they could enforce a settlement on their terms. If it was bad for Pickford it was far worse for those who depended upon him. As bricklayers, and their like, were not articulate men it is rare we hear their point of view. The *Derby Mercury* records one sad case of a nameless mason who hanged himself in the backyard of The George after drinking away all he possessed, but this was printed more as a warning against the evils of drink than as a sympathetic tribute to a poor man who had fallen on hard times.

On the other hand, building workers were skilled tradesmen who had served a seven-year apprenticeship, and in theory at least had the opportunity to achieve the status of independent master craftsmen. Of the thirty-three masons, bricklayers and joiners who worked on the Derby Assembly Rooms[4] in 1763–4 and were paid by the day, only one, Thomas Gardner, achieved the status of an architect builder. Though the three Eglington brothers, Benjamin, Samuel and Timothy, were related to a successful family of builders in the Birmingham, Coventry area, Samuel Eglington settled in Ashbourne, where, assisted by his wife and daughters, he combined the business of carving gravestones with that of a shopkeeper. Though far from satisfactory at least the family were able to stay together and eke out some kind of living.

The rates of pay for building workers, though not princely, compared favourably with those of other trades. To return again to the building of the Derby Assembly Rooms: the masons received between 2s. and 2s. 6d. a day, the bricklayers and joiners slightly less; the labourers, up to twenty in number at any one time, were paid 1s. a day, the same as a common foot soldier, though two or three, who were probably more able, were given a penny or two more. Though the outdoor life of a building tradesman was preferable to that of a mill worker, the very nature of their work meant that they were constantly on the move seeking fresh employment. This did not encourage a settled home life, and probably explains why masons were regarded as notorious drinkers.

Josiah Wedgwood, in a letter to his partner, details Pickford's method of working as the architect himself recounted it:[5]

Mr Pickford promised before he left to send me the particulars, [a detailed breakdown of the price] he s'd he thought it not right to give such things to Noblemen and Gent'n as it hurt the neighbourhood, for the Gent'n wo'd afterwards expect his tenants etc. to work for him as low as they did for the undertakers w'ch was not reasonable, as a Gent'n will not consider and allow for a mischance, or bad bargain like a workman, and seldom pay so well. At the same time he assured me that he w'ld do my building upon very different [much lower] terms than he did for Gent'n.

In such a moral climate it is not surprising that their relationship should terminate in an acrimonious dispute, recounted later in these pages.

When Pickford died he left a comfortable fortune for his widow and children, but there is little doubt that he had to work for it. He was no gentleman, and for him architecture was not a gentleman's profession. Today things are different, or are they? Now the name 'architect' can only be used by people registered with ARCUK (Architects Registration Council United Kingdom) which in effect means they have passed the examinations of the RIBA. Non members who wish to practice are forced to describe themselves as 'architectural consultants', or some other title that does not contravene the law. But as the government now proposes to abolish ARCUK, and architect will no longer be a protected name, we shall shortly be back to a situation all too familiar to Joseph Pickford.

Nevertheless, Pickford always insisted upon being called 'architect', even though the editor of the *Derby Mercury*, either through spite, or ignorance, never rated him as more than an 'eminent builder'.[6] But still, in the end did this matter? Fine birds are always recognized by their plumage, and few in the provinces came finer than Joseph Pickford.

PART TWO:

THE BUILDINGS

CHAPTER FOUR

Early Associations

Some time after the autumn of 1756 the young Joseph Pickford returned to his native Warwickshire. His brother and sisters were still living in the area, but it was not his intention to settle there. Like his father and uncles before him he took employment as a clerk of works, not as a full-time occupation, but as a stepping stone to establish his own career.

William Hiorne (*c.* 1712–76), and his brother David who died in 1758, were by this time the principal architect builders in Warwick.[1] The last of the Smith family, William Smith, died unmarried in 1747, and what evidence there is suggests that the Hiorne brothers succeeded to his business. It would appear that Pickford's first employment was supervising the building of Foremark Hall in Derbyshire, a house designed by David Hiorne for Sir Robert Burdett.[2]

Although David Hiorne died before work on the building began there is no

Foremark Hall, Derbyshire

Foremark Hall, Derbyshire

doubt that he was the architect. Dr Andor Gomme, an authority on the work of Francis Smith of Warwick and his successors, is of the opinion that his brother William Hiorne was also a competent designer of country houses and was quite capable of settling the final design after his brother's death. Wolfe and Gandon in volume V of *Vitruvius Britannicus*, published in 1771, duck the issue by simply naming 'Hiorns' as the architect of Foremark Hall.[3]

To control the building of a large country house like Foremark was an excellent training for a young man who had ambitions to succeed on his own. Pickford's masters in Warwick were a day's ride away, so the whole responsibility for organizing the labour and materials would have fallen upon him. We have no knowledge of Pickford's terms of employment, but we do know that while the work was going on he had sufficient freedom to seek out potential clients with a view to setting up his own practice.

Sir Robert Burdett, the 4th Baronet, was Hiorne's patron. His family had owned the estate since the seventeenth century, but their house, though large and convenient, was in need of rebuilding. This, Sir Robert decided to do in 1758,[4] when the family moved to Knowle Hill near Ticknall, about two miles from Foremark, until the new building was ready. The design he chose was a conventional Palladian mansion based on Isaac Ware's Wrotham Park in Middlesex, built a few years earlier in 1754,[5] though Foremark, reduced in scale, makes a less satisfactory composition.

The best contemporary account of the house comes from that inveterate traveller, John Byng, later the 5th Viscount Torrington.[6] How he acquired his architectural expertise is not clear as by profession he was a soldier, Colonel of the Foot Guards. But in middle life, between 1781 and 1794, he chose to make a number of tours through England, recording everything of interest in his journal.

Byng was deeply conservative, and deeply prejudiced. He preferred the old to the new, especially in architecture. He loathed the enclosure of the fields, then going on apace, as much as we today loathe the destruction of the hedgerows. He was a natural conservationist, and thoroughly disliked newfangled fashions, absentee parsons and landlords, Scotch firs, turnpike roads, and landscape gardeners and their improvements, 'to be put under taste by Mr Repton', he called it, though in this matter his impartiality is open to question as at one point he refers to 'our good friend Lancelot Brown'. Yet he was an acute observer of all that passed his gaze, and by and large his observations display sound common sense.

Although he was most uncomplimentary about Foremark Hall, which was then stark and relatively new, he was delighted with Anchor church, a hermit's cell close by on the banks of the River Trent.

Keeping the hill top, I was soon directed to the rocks, called Anchor-church, above which, leaving my horses at the wicket gate, I walk'd thro' a small wood . . . and by a steep descent of turf steps, to this picturesque scenery of delight: and where, even, sequestration and anchoritism might appear happiness: of all men I shou'd prove one of the fittest for such a plan; my pleasures are few, and I cou'd catch and dress my fish.[7]

Anchor church, Ingleby, Derbyshire

And then in sharp contrast:

> About a mile from this pleasant, happy spot, stands Foremark, a house built within these 30 years by Sir Robert Burdett; which is of vile architecture, and in a bad situation; in front there is a paltry pond, with pitiful plantations: I never wish to enter these Venetian vanities.[8]

Although his indictment of the 'vile architecture' is more an expression of his prejudice than an architectural criticism we can understand his feelings, as even today Anchor church has an enchantment that Foremark Hall lacks.

One understands his lack of feeling for, what was for him, modern architecture, but it is difficult to accept his description of the park without comment. Foremark was not a new estate. In 1713 Woolley commented that it had been added to with 'a great deal of art which renders it a most delightful place'.[9] Taste changes, and Woolley's notion of the ideal was not the same as the received opinion in Hiorne's day, but it is difficult to believe that all its former beauty had been destroyed.

The 'paltry pond, with pitiful plantations', were the work of the eminent landscape architect, William Emes (1729–1803) who laid out the park in 1759–61, but as he was also responsible for beautifying Anchor church, perhaps he can be forgiven.[10] Emes began his working life as gardener to Lord Scarsdale at Kedleston, and Foremark was one of his earliest commissions. Over the next twenty years he worked with Pickford on many of his projects, but it was at Foremark that they first became acquainted.

Although we do not claim that Pickford had any part in the design of Foremark Hall, as clerk of works he almost certainly made a contribution to the detail. The Ionic door surround on the garden front is still as crisp as the day it was carved, and a credit to Pickford and the masons under his control. Unfortunately their names are not recorded, but undoubtedly they were the same men who worked for Pickford on his own contracts later.

Apart from the Hall other work was carried out on the estate at the same time, in particular Knowle Hill which was demolished and rebuilt as a romantic retreat.[11] The summer-house range appears to have been part of Hiorne's work and presumably Pickford was responsible for building it, but the sad ruin the visitor sees today is only the remains of a much larger house. Still, the pretty Gothick windows and the Ashford black marble chimney piece gives some idea of what the building was like.

Another house on the estate, built at the same time, was Ingleby Toft, the residence of Robert Greaves, Sir Robert Burdett's agent. It has a handsome redbrick façade with stone dressings which Dr Gomme believes was designed by the Hiorne brothers. Robert Greaves was the brother of Joseph of Aston Lodge[12] who we know had business dealings with Pickford a few years later, which suggests that he, too, was probably involved with the building, though it is doubtful that he was the architect.

We know that Pickford worked at Foremark from the middle of 1759 until at least December 1760, more or less the whole contract period. We now know that apart from supervising the work there, he was also seeking to further his own career. His earliest known letter is post dated, 'Foremark, Decemb. 6th 1760',[13] and is addressed to Matthew Boulton at Snow Hill. Ostensibly it was written to introduce the bearer to a brickmaker, named Hibbeard, but in reality he was pushing his services as an architect. He concludes, 'I will take care to get you some sketches made for your new house very soon which I hope you will find agreeable.'

Presumably this was an unsolicited design for Soho House in Birmingham, and though the house was built shortly afterwards it is not clear who was the architect. Timothy Lightoler began construction of the Soho manufactory in 1761,[14] but was superseded by Benjamin Wyatt & Co. about 1765.[15] Wyatt and his sons were also responsible for the completion of Soho House, but the original architect seems to have been either Lightoler or Pickford.

Around the spring of 1761, Pickford left Foremark and moved to Derby, because by this date he had settled on his future bride. She was Mary Wilkins, the daughter of the agent to Wenman Coke of Longford Hall, Pickford's first and principal patron. It is possible that Mary had a special place in Coke's affection, but whatever the reason, he was a staunch friend to Pickford in the years to come.[16]

This first undertaking, the remodelling of Longford Hall, must have been started some time in 1761, but the only reference we have to it is contained in a letter Pickford wrote to Ralph Sneyd, of Keele Hall in Staffordshire, on 13 May 1762:

> I have some very sober good masons which I should be very glad to send to prepare stone ready in forwardness for the Building. They are now at Mr Cokes of Longford, and have nearly compleated the stonework there.[17]

Pickford's work at Longford would not have met with the approval of Lord Torrington, for what he did was to turn a gabled Tudor manor-house into a rather inadequate regular classical façade. The proportions were far from satisfactory, and to make matters worse the old house had a range of chimney-stacks on the external wall facing the garden, which somehow had to be accommodated.

Pickford's answer was to raise the building another storey, with a blank screen wall topped off with a Doric frieze and a stone balustrade. To complete the transformation, sash windows were added to the ground and first floors. Though he could not hide the chimneys he at least reduced their prominence

Longford Hall, Longford, Derbyshire

by incorporating them into a balustrade. But once the decision was taken to keep the chimneys, the result was certain to be an awkward compromise. Externally Longford Hall stands today much as Pickford left it, though earlier this century the interior was destroyed by fire and it is now greatly changed.

There is one other building at Longford which is probably the work of Pickford, that is the fine stable block in redbrick that stands close by. This being newly built it is all of a piece and has none of the imperfections of the Hall. The simple brick construction and the excellence of the proportions gives it a dignity which is totally lacking in the main house.

As at Longford, the other architectural proposals Pickford made at this time to Ralph Sneyd were for remodelling an earlier house. The Sneyd family had been established in Staffordshire since the fifteenth century, and built the first Keele Hall about 1580.[18] They were a cultivated family, more devoted to their interests in the county than politics, which probably explains why they were never ennobled. By 1761 Keele Hall must have been in need of modernization, but such ideas were eventually set aside as nothing of consequence was done until the nineteenth century, when Salvin was employed to build the house we see today at the centre of Keele University.

Pickford's proposals, dated August 1761,[19] were for taking down and rebuilding part of the house, and for new offices. The house was to be remodelled in stone from a local quarry, and though we have no idea what form the design took, the letter suggests a modification by carrying up the 'bow windows' to the attic to improve the 'look out'. Apparently, the original idea had been to hide the attic windows behind the parapet wall, a device Pickford was later to use at Dr Taylor's house in Ashbourne.

The sum quoted for the alterations to the house was £648 17s. 6d., and the price for the offices in redbrick with a tiled roof was £786 17s. 8d.[20] Though not expensive it was too much for Ralph Sneyd. In the end all of Pickford's endeavours at Keele came to nothing, it was another job to put down to experience.

It is not known how many of these early schemes were commissioned, and how many were merely speculations which Pickford attempted to foist on to potential clients, but by far the most interesting is the design for a new house he sent to Sir Henry Harpur of Calke.[21] This was discovered by Howard Colvin rolled up behind a bookcase in the library at Calke Abbey, and though the drawings are not signed they are without doubt the work of Pickford.

The history of Calke Abbey and the eccentricities of its owners are so well documented in Colvin's excellent book[22] that it is unnecessary to retell the story here, except to recount the part played in it by Joseph Pickford. The gloomy mansion built by Sir John Harpur at the beginning of the eighteenth century was not known as Calke Abbey until 1808. Before then it was called Calke Hall, or Calke House, with the more usual spelling as Caulk, which goes some way towards explaining the pronunciation of the name.

Sir John's grandson, Sir Henry Harpur, called Harry, came of age in 1760, and amid great rejoicing took possession of 'Caulk Hall and the estate'. Two years later he made a fashionable marriage with the Earl of Warwick's daughter, Lady Frances Greville, and with an income approaching £10,000 a year was well placed to indulge his fancies. These for the most part centred around racehorses, but in 1761 he was returned to Parliament for the county of Derby and retained the seat until the election of 1768.

Like all the fashionable gentry the Harpurs had a house in London where they spent much of their time. Yet their estate in Derbyshire must have been of interest to them, or at least Pickford thought so, or he would not have wasted his time preparing a set of drawings for a new house. There are no account books at Calke for the period from 1760 until 1772, not that we would expect to find a payment to Pickford for the designs, but the few bills and scraps that have survived show that Pickford was in constant employment there during that decade, so his efforts were not entirely wasted.

In 1768 he was paid for building the Riding School[23] which is attached to the stables at the rear of the house. It is a plain, barn-like structure in redbrick with a blue tile roof in the vernacular style of the area, with no architectural pretensions save for a great Diocletian window in the end gable. In the same year he also submitted a bill for resashing the windows in the house and slating the church roof.[24]

The drawings are not dated or signed, but it is most likely they were presented to Sir Harry shortly after his marriage, some time between 1762 and 1764, when Pickford was still working on the Derby Assembly Rooms to which Sir Harry subscribed. Whatever the date it must have been before the windows were resashed as no one would spend money on a house about to be pulled down.

The handwriting on the drawing is the formal copperplate style, typical of Pickford and many other architects of the period, but the inconsistencies in the spelling and the form of the captions are peculiar to the Derby architect. Of the spelling we are given both 'dining' and 'dineing', as well as 'Principall Story' and 'Anti-Room', all mistakes which he makes elsewhere. Turning to the captions, the heading to the main front reads: 'An Elevation of a House and Offices design'd for Sir Henry Harpur Bart. at Caulk in Derbyshire.' Compare this with 'Elevation of the Moot Hall design'd to be Built at Wirksworth in Derbyshire',[25] or 'A Rough Sketch of a window design'd for St Mary's church in Nottingham'.[26]

As far as we know Pickford never designed another house on quite this scale, but there are elements in other buildings which are repeated on the drawings at Calke. Two features on the main elevation strike an immediate chord. The urns on the balustrade are identical in form to those at St Helen's House in Derby, and the end bays are stepped forward in a similar fashion to both Ogston Hall and Etruria. It must be said that although the design has considerable merit, it appears to be the work of a man not used to handling

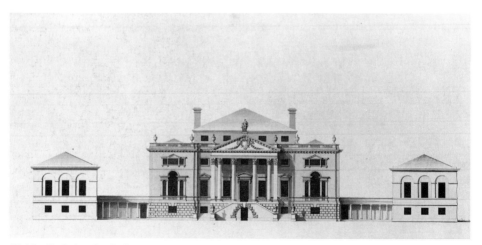

Pickford's design for Calke Abbey

buildings on a large scale. This is particularly true of the garden façade which is so badly thought out, it would have served Pickford's purpose better if he had omitted it altogether.

The design is for a typical Palladian villa, with the main house linked to the service wings with quadrant colonnades. The central block is dominated by the Great Hall in the form of a double cube. This is at first-floor level with access from the outside by a handsome perron surmounted by a Corinthian portico the full height of the building.

To Pickford's credit, the portico is more lively than the usual Palladian affair. The square pillars at the corners look back to Inigo Jones' design for old St Paul's Cathedral. This was taken down after the Great Fire of London, so Pickford could not have seen it himself, but what he did see was Isaac Ware's edition of *Palladio's I Quattro Libri dell' Architettura*, published in London in 1738, to which Joseph Pickford senior subscribed.

In Book IV, devoted to ancient temples, Palladio illustrates the so-called 'Temple of Clitumnus' between Foligno and Spoleto, near Trevi. This has a similar Corinthian portico to the one shown on the design for the new house at Calke. Similar that is in elevation, because the corner pillars at Trevi are joined to the side walls of the temple cella. Palladio introduces the idea again in Book II, on plate XIX, only on this occasion as a colonnade to the loggia of a great house.

This is not to suggest that Pickford was a slave to Palladio. The main front of Sir Harry's house looks back to Colen Campbell's designs for Houghton in Norfolk, not Vicenza. For instance, the architectural motif most associated with Palladio is the three-light Venetian window, which he used to great effect

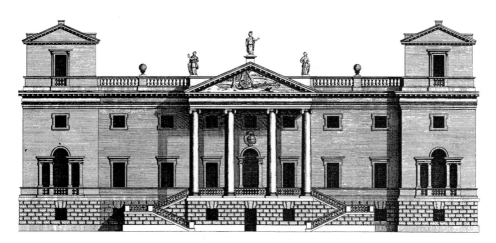

Houghton Hall, Norfolk

as an open arcade. The way Pickford used it as a feature window in a solid wall was an English development hardly understood in Italy.

It will suffice to show Campbell's south front at Houghton beside Pickford's principal façade for the reader to understand the point at issue. Campbell's scheme is nine-bays wide, Pickford's is seven. Campbell raised the projecting end bays by one storey, whereas Pickford carried these through at the level of the portico with a raised attic storey in the centre. Apart from that, the concept is the same. Professor Wittkower tells us: 'The grouping of Houghton was repeated with slight modifications in the most notable country houses for more than a generation.'[27] If Sir Harry had been expecting a design in the latest fashion he would not have been impressed.

With the plans and elevations of the house is a detailed design for the dining room, which shows what Pickford could have achieved if his clients had been sufficiently endowed. It is an essay in the popular Palladian rococo style of the day. It is drawn in the usual eighteenth-century manner, with the four elevations laid out flat on the ground plan, like a child's paper cut-out waiting to be assembled. This is a method of drawing not much used today, but it has many advantages as it shows at a glance the four walls in juxtaposition.

Without doubt it would have been an elegant room; but the pier glasses, the acanthus scrolls in the plaster frieze and the chimney-piece, all date from the previous generation. Only the view of a wild romantic landscape in the overmantel suggests a contemporary theme, and this might have been drawn with Joseph Wright in mind.

If this scheme marked the end of the first phase of Pickford's professional life, then he could look back with some satisfaction, for a young architect starting from scratch with little capital had no alternative but to shower the gentry with unsolicited schemes in the hope that one might fall on fertile ground. As these designs cost him nothing but his time, he could afford to speculate in this manner, at least to begin with, but it was no way for an ambitious man to conduct his business on a long-term basis. Fortunately for Pickford, Wenman Coke came to his aid, but even without him, there is no doubt that with his drive, Pickford would have succeeded eventually.

CHAPTER FIVE

The Derby Assembly Rooms

The gentlemen's assemblies, which met in every county town, were one of the great civilizing forces in eighteenth-century England. Their purpose was to inculcate the social graces, encourage the liberal arts, and bring together all sorts and conditions of men on equal footing. In theory they were outside politics, a neutral ground where political rivals could meet, and for the time being discuss matters of mutual interest and seek the common good.

Beau Nash, speaking of the assembly at Tunbridge Wells, summed up the idea perfectly: 'People of the greatest title, rank and dignity, people of every learned profession, of every Religion and Political persuasion; people of every degree, condition and occupation of life, (if well dressed and well behaved) meet amicably here together.'[1] For such notions to flourish a new kind of meeting room was needed. By common consent the greatest of the English assembly rooms is at York, built between 1731 and 1732.

The architect for the York Assembly Rooms was Richard Boyle, 3rd Earl of Burlington, a Yorkshire nobleman, whose 'mission [in life] was to reinstate in England the canons of Roman Architecture as described by Vitruvius, exemplified by its surviving remains, and practiced by Palladio, Scamozzi, and [Inigo] Jones'. In this he was largely successful, nowhere more so than in the Assembly Rooms at York, with its magnificent 'Egyptian Hall' of close-set columns.[2]

The foundation stone proclaimed that it was a 'place for public pastime where liberal arts should flourish and where new splendour should emulate the ancient glory of Eboracum'. Though the sentiments concerning Roman York were tenets of faith held to be true mainly by Yorkshiremen, the belief that their city had its roots in an ancient tradition going back to Roman times was certainly correct.

By 1762 Derby, a town of similar size to York, was in desperate need of a common meeting place. In some ways it was better situated than York; as Daniel Defoe had noted, in Derbyshire more of the gentry resided close to the county town than was usual. He thought they gathered there for greater comfort, because the county was such 'a howling wilderness', but whatever the reason, the county certainly needed an elegant room where the gentry could meet on equal footing.[3]

The Assembly Rooms, York

Since the early eighteenth century there had been two assemblies in Derby, one for the gentry and another for the townspeople. In the 1740s the principal assembly for the gentry was presided over by Mrs Barnes, known as 'Blowzabella', the wife of a Derbyshire gentleman of small fortune. Whether she would have agreed with Beau Nash on the make-up of the ideal assembly is open to question, but the one anecdote we know about her would suggest otherwise. In 1752, when her reign finally came to an end, she handed over the account book to Lady Ferrers containing a note, 'I told her that Trade never mix'd with Us Ladies.'[4]

Alas, this was not an attitude limited to families of small fortune. It would seem that even ladies of rank thought much the same. There survives from the 1730s a list of 'Rules to be observed in the Ladies Assembly in Derby'. These include such conditions as '1. No Attorney's Clerk shall be admitted. 2. No Shopkeeper, or any of his or her family shall be admitted, except Mr Franceys'.[5] It is not known for certain why Mr Franceys was so favoured, but of all the explanations we prefer the one that as apothecary to the gentry he knew too many of their medical secrets.

Fortunately not everyone was so narrow-minded and constricted by attitudes of class. Lady Jane Coke, for one, argued for a broader mix of people. She gave as her opinion: 'Tis hard out of two Assemblies you have at Derby people can't agree to make one good one.' But no positive action was taken until the ladies were reduced to dancing with each other.[6]

As always in Derbyshire it was the Duke of Devonshire who took the lead. With his initiative a building committee was formed, and a subscription list opened.[7] As architectural adviser they selected one of their own number, Washington Shirley, 5th Earl Ferrers (1722–88), a gifted amateur, who is also reputed to have designed his own house, Staunton Harold Hall in Leicestershire.[8] He, in turn, appointed Joseph Pickford to supervise the construction and organize the labour, though how far Pickford's duties extended is not made clear in the account book.[9] Still, this accords with what little we know about Ferrers, as at Staunton Harold he employed another young aspiring architect, William Henderson of Loughborough, in the same position.[10]

There can be no doubt that Earl Ferrers was a man of exceptional gifts. He served in the navy where he rose to the rank of Vice Admiral. In 1761 he was elected a Fellow of the Royal Society, and in 1775 he was an honorary exhibitor at the Royal Academy, showing three sectional drawings of different vessels designed by himself.[11] As a patron of the arts he commissioned Joseph Wright's masterpiece, *A Philosopher giving a lecture on the Orrery*, which hung for many years at Staunton Harold, before it was acquired by the Derby Art Gallery.[12]

If Earl Ferrers ever aspired to be an architect we only have the word of Throsby and Nichols for it, as it was they who stated in their respective histories of Leicestershire that he was responsible for the design of Staunton Harold Hall. Their motive for making this claim could not have been the wish to flatter a potential patron, as Ferrers died in 1788, and Throsby did not publish until the following year, and Nichols not until 1804. Nichols in particular was a most reliable historian and it is doubtful if he would have made such a claim without seeing some evidence or speaking to a trustworthy witness. We must take it then that Earl Ferrers, as an enthusiastic amateur architect, was responsible for the design of the Derby Assembly Rooms.

Both of these buildings are distinctly old-fashioned in design, but this would seem natural if the architect had spent most of his life at sea. What we know of Earl Ferrers suggests that he was a dilettante with a genuine interest in many subjects, but with no great depth of knowledge in any particular one. This was certainly true of architecture as it now seems that both of the designs attributed to him were, in part, the work of others.

This is plain to see from a close examination of the stonework sections on both buildings. The window surrounds on the Full Street elevation of the Assembly Rooms were exactly the same as those on Pickford's own house in Friar Gate, but how much of the final design was due to Pickford rather than Earl Ferrers is unknown. Pickford probably worked up a simple sketch by Ferrers into a practical design drawing for his men, including in it some ideas of his own.

Such a method of working might flatter the ego of a gentleman amateur, but it contains many pitfalls, most of which came to light at the Assembly Rooms. It is essential in any undertaking involving the expenditure of money that the person in charge understands his business and does not rely upon his subordinates for essential knowledge.

The Assembly Rooms, Derby

It seems fairly certain from the account book that the contractual method suggested by Pickford to Ralph Sneyd, what is known today as 'cost plus', was adopted at Derby. By this system the contractor finds the labour and materials, but is not responsible for the overall cost. With our knowledge of the people involved and with a fixed amount of money to spend the outcome was inevitable. There is no doubt that Pickford did a good job until the money ran out, but due to the failure of Earl Ferrers to control the expenditure nine years were to elapse before the interior of the building was finally completed by Robert Adam.[13] But this was all in the future. For the present everyone was satisfied with their architect and his young assistant.

We do not know if the gentlemen on the committee approved a design brief, but the one for the York Assembly Rooms, sent to Lord Burlington in 1730, has survived:

What is wanted is a large Dancing Room, not less than ninety feet long, another large room for cards and play, another for coffee and refreshments and a kitchen or place to make tea in, with a Retiring place for the Ladies. And somewhere about the entrance, perhaps underground, a place with a chimney for footmen.[14]

An Acc.t of the Gentlemens Subscribers, to the Assembly Room in Derby

	£. s. d
His Grace the Duke of Devonshire	100.0.0
Sir Henry Harpur Bar.t	200
Earl Ferrers	52.10
Sir Robert Burdett Bar.t	50
William Fitzherbert Esq.r	100
Wenman Coke Esq.r	30
Hugo Meynell Esq.r	30
Sir Hen.r Hunloke Bar.t	50
Philip Gell Esq.r	21
Francis Munday Esq.r	21
Joseph Greaves Esq.r	10.10
Edward Munday Esq.r	21
Rich.d Fitzherbert Esq.r	10.15
Rob.t Mead Wilmot Esq.r	10.15
Garman Poll Esq.r	30
H. W. Mortimer Esq.r	10.10
Geo. Morewood Esq.r	21
H. Coape Esq.r	21
Jn.o Gisborne Esq.r	40
Sam.u Crompton Esq.r	30
Lord Vernon	100
Will.m Cotton Esq.r	10.10
Sir John Every Bar.t	21
Godfrey Clarke Esq.r	100
M.r B: Hodgson	10
J. Shuttleworth Esq.r	20
Sam.u Shore Esq.r	21
R. Newton Esq.r	30
Tho.s Bainbrigge Esq.r	10.10
The Corporation	31.10
Sir Rob.t Wilmot	25
His Grace the Duke of Norfolk	100
Lord C. Cavendish	30
Rich.d Beresford Esq.r	10.10
John Lowe Esq.r	21
C. Horton Esq.r	5.5
R. B: Hodghimson Esq.r	30
Leo Fosbrook Esq.r	21
Exuperius Turner Esq.r	2.2
£	1759.7.0

The Subscription List for the Derby Assembly Rooms

Doubtless the requirements at Derby were similar, but the disposition of the rooms was different. The main hall for dancing was at first-floor level with a retiring area to one side. Beyond that in a separate building were the supper rooms. The room for card playing, obligatory at any assembly, was probably on the ground floor with the footmen's chimney and 'the necessary', but this area was completely rearranged in modern times and no plans have survived to show the original layout.

The authority for Pickford's involvement is the account book signed by him and written in his own hand. At least two copies have survived, one in the archive of William FitzHerbert of Tissington, the Recorder for Derby. It is a complete and comprehensive document giving not only the names of all the workmen employed, but the work they did and the time it took them to perform the task. It is by far the best account of any undertaking that Pickford was ever engaged on.

Preparation work began on site in July 1762, when Pickford sent his 'good, sober masons' under their foreman Benjamin Eglington to get stone ready for the building. Eglington, like Pickford, belonged to a family who were later to gain a considerable reputation in the midland counties as mason architects. It is believed they came from Badby in Northamptonshire, and at least three of the brothers, Benjamin, Samuel and Timothy worked on the Assembly Rooms and other contracts for Pickford. Benjamin died young and was buried at St Werburgh's church in Derby in August 1768. Samuel settled in Ashbourne where a gravestone signed by him can still be seen by the footpath leading to the south door of the church.

On 18 February 1763 the *Derby Mercury* recorded: 'This morning the workmen began to pull down the Blackamoor's Head and the adjoining house in the Market Place in order to build the Grand Assembly Room'. This is confirmed by the account book which shows seventeen labourers taken on at a shilling a day. Three weeks later, on 11 March, Earl Ferrers, attended by the mayor, laid the foundation stone and the workmen were given 'a handsome present'.

All that year building continued. The workforce varied in number, but in the summer months, when the days were longest, it reached as many as forty-five. The wages paid to the men ranged from 3s. 6d. a day for the foreman, Benjamin Eglington, to between 1s. and 1s. 6d. for labourers, depending upon their age and ability. Tradesmen received between 2s. and 3s., with the higher rates generally going to the masons rather than the joiners. Among the latter was Thomas Gardner, a 26-year-old joiner, paid 2s. a day. After the work on the Assembly Rooms was finished Pickford took him on as an assistant. Gardner stayed with Pickford for nearly ten years, and when he left he set up his own business as an architect in Uttoxeter, which he continued until his death in 1804.

The progress on the main front that faced on to the Market Place is easy to follow. By the middle of April the rustic base had reached door-head height. A month later payment was made for the Ionic surrounds to the first-floor windows, and in June work began on the modillion cornice. By September the shell of the building was complete and the workforce dropped to single figures.

The bas-relief in the pediment, presumably designed by Pickford, depicting an assortment of musical instruments was carved by Mr Radcliffe. No other detail is given, but he was probably the Nottingham carver noted by Rupert Gunnis.[15] Radcliffe had business ties with the architect Samuel Stretton, and may also have worked for Pickford on the Nottingham County Hall.

The final payment was made on 2 June 1764, when the total monies disbursed for labour amounted to £755 14s. Benjamin Eglington, who was present when the work started, was the last to be paid off. To be added to this amount were the bills of the subcontractors and suppliers of £1,198 7s. 6d. plus the unpaid bills of £329 3s. 10d., giving a grand total of £2,283 5s. 3d. To meet these charges the subscribers had promised £1,759 7s. which, added to the receipts for old materials, left a shortfall of £513 15s. 9d. If Pickford was in any way to blame for this sorry state of affairs the gentlemen on the committee made no attempt to dock his wages, as the final payment in the book was to the assistant architect. 'For my time and trouble as agreed with Earl Ferrers £100.'

Nothing more is heard for over a year until 6 September 1765, when the *Derby Mercury* reported that, 'On Tuesday night the new Assembly Room was opened for the first time, when there was a brilliant assembly of ladies and gentlemen . . . we are assured the additional subscription made towards completing the said building amounted to £750.' So there we have it, the day

The Assembly Rooms, Derby

was saved by the long suffering gentlemen subscribers, but as no more is heard of Earl Ferrers we must assume he relinquished his responsibilities.

The finishes to the interior, such as they were, were only a temporary expedient, until the gentlemen knew what they wanted and where the money was coming from to pay for it. Five years passed before matters came to a head with an advertisement in the *Derby Mercury* on 30 November 1770:

> That the gentlemen appointed to superintend the finishing of the County Assembly Rooms at Derby intend to meet at the King's Head on Thursday December 20th. All persons who intend to produce plans to finish the same are desired to bring them to us at this meeting as an agreement will be entered into with one of them that the said rooms may be complete by the next races.

It is very doubtful if they expected this to produce what they were looking for as a month earlier they had persuaded Lord Scarsdale to write to Robert Adam.

> The gentlemen of Derby have decided to finish the inside of the Assembly Room immediately. We should therefore be much obliged to you for a design and estimate of the finishing. I understand it is not to be highly ornamented and the stucco work is to be executed by Mr Denstone of Derby. I find they have had some designs which they disliked. I think it will require great skill to manage the musick gallery so as not to be very ugly, for if it is sunk into the wall the musick will not be heard and if the cove is not well managed I fear the echo will be offensive and troublesome. The proportions of the room appear to me to be very awkward. The Gazetteer mentions where the drawings are lodged. I beg the favour of an answer by the posts return.

A few days later James Adam replied to say his brother was out of town, but they would be pleased to undertake the commission:

> I never saw the Assembly Rooms in Derby, but from your Lordships description I imagine there must be a good deal of difficulty to manage it cleverly, however I never saw a room so awkward that something good could be made of it. Tis the business of Art to overcome difficulty and I make no doubt that we shall be able to overcome them in the present case.

On 1 December 1770 Robert Adam himself wrote a letter to Lord Scarsdale, which partly explains why the gentlemen quietly abandoned their plan to have the rooms finished in time for the race week in September 1771:

. . . These circumstances have put it out of our power of getting anything done to the design of the Assembly Room in Derby. I find by your Lordships letter . . . that the meeting relative to that affair is put off for about ten days. But that is too short a time to do anything clever or to make out drawings of it which are of a tedious and laborious kind. If the Gentlemen concerned would allow sufficient time for making and considering the different designs of the ceilings and sidewalls I would with great pleasure do my best for them and the Holidays will be the only leizure time I could have to do them and myself justice as I should be sorry to lay any undigested thing before them.

Robert Adam was as good as his word and completed his designs by 30 July 1771, when another advertisement in the *Derby Mercury* stated that 'A plan for finishing the building has been fixed upon at the assizes and that persons

The interior of the Derby Assembly Rooms

wishing to contract for the work should have their estimates ready by September 3rd.'

All now appeared to be plain sailing, yet three more years passed before the final triumph in September 1774. Neither the letters at Kedleston nor the *Derby Mercury* suggest any reason for this delay, though it would be no surprise to learn that after so many false dawns the gentlemen were beginning to jib at the cost. It was clearly a case of taking the bucket to the well once too often.

Adam's answer to the awkward shape of the interior was to form the ceiling as a barrel vault running the full length of the ballroom bringing the cornice down to a manageable level. The music gallery he positioned over the entrance in the centre of the long side, though in modern times the band always played in the body of the hall. The plasterwork on the ceiling was all the gentlemen could have desired, a low relief neo-classical design worked with great skill by Abraham Denstone, Derby's principal plasterer.

Denstone was an excellent choice for the job because he had worked for some years at Kedleston, and was well equipped to produce the quality of work Adam expected. It is a pity we know so little about him; he probably worked with Joseph Pickford elsewhere but no records survive to prove it. He was undoubtedly successful because at his death in 1779, apart from his own

The interior of the Derby Assembly Rooms

house in St Mary's Gate, he owned The Mitre in Full Street, another house in Walker Lane and the brickworks at Rowditch Farm. His father, also Abraham, had been a plasterer before him and was responsible for the plasterwork at the Guild Hall in 1731–2. His brother James described himself as an architect and possibly designed Markeaton Hall, the seat of the Mundy family, near Derby.[16]

All we know of Abraham's personal life are the facts of his death. On 25 March 1779 the *Derby Mercury* informs us that: 'Yesterday morning about 7 o'clock died after a few hours illness of gout in the stomach, Mr Abraham Denstone, plasterer, in the St Mary's Gate.' Modern medical opinion suggests the cause of his death was probably peritonitis.

At the race week in September 1774 the grand opening so long awaited finally took place. It was a sight to remember, or at least the *Derby Mercury* thought so:

> The company on Tuesday night at the new assembly rooms was very numerous and more brilliant than we scarce ever remember, amongst the nobility present were their Graces the Duke and Duchess of Devonshire, the Countess Spencer with her son and daughter, Lord Althorpe and Harriet Spencer, Lord Vernon etc. etc. The minuets were opened by the Hon. Mr Greville and her Grace the Duchess of Devonshire.

How satisfying it would be if that was the end of the story. By any standard the Derby Assembly Rooms with its elegant ballroom was a fine building, though in the end nobody lifted a finger to save it when the Corporation decided to redevelop the north side of the Market Place. A minor fire caused by a workman's blowlamp provided the excuse for demolition in 1963, but it would have gone anyway once the decision to build the new Assembly Rooms was taken. As a sop to local opinion the old façade that had looked out on to the square for two hundred years, and on which Pickford and his workmen had lavished so much attention, was taken down and re-erected at the Crich Tramway Museum. A more inappropriate place it would be hard to imagine, but it saved the Corporation from having to break it up for road metal.

CHAPTER SIX

Early Work in Ashbourne and District

Derbyshire, more than most counties, has great variations in scenery. Limestone crags and stone walls give way to hedgerows and green fields with an abruptness that even surprises the people who know the district well. Ashbourne, a mile from the Staffordshire border, sits on the divide. The buildings in the town reflect its geographical position, being part brick and part stone, with an abundance of blue tile roofs.

In the eighteenth century, the principal families in the area were all related by marriage; among them were the Boothbys, the Beresfords, the Okeovers, the Meynells of Bradley, and the FitzHerberts of Tissington. So it seems only natural that if one of them should have his house rebuilt, the others would follow soon after and probably use the same architect.

Dr John Taylor (1711–88), who lived at the Mansion in Church Street, is best remembered as being the close friend of Dr Johnson. They were an odd pair. Politically they were poles apart, with little in common save for their boyhood memories. Johnson humorously depicted his Derbyshire friend's conversation as being chiefly concerned with bulls and country matters. Yet when the summer came he invariably thought of him and frequently made the journey north to Ashbourne, on the last occasion, only a few months before he died.[1]

To suppose Ashbourne was all 'bulls and country matters' would be a great mistake. In 1766 Jean Jacques Rousseau was brought to England by David Hume and settled nearby at Wootton Hall, where it is said the locals knew him as 'owd Ross Hall'.[2] Exactly what effect his revolutionary philosophy had on the gentry thereabouts is difficult to say, but his interest in botany certainly inspired the young Brooke Boothby and Dr Erasmus Darwin to form the Lichfield Botanical Society in 1778.[3]

The most permanent monument to Rousseau's stay is his *Dialogues*, a biographical work written after his return to France. Brooke Boothby brought the manuscript back to England from Paris at Rousseau's request and published it in Lichfield in 1780. The following year Wright painted the famous portrait of Boothby reclining in a wood with the volume under his hand.[4]

How Pickford obtained his introduction to Ashbourne society can only be guessed at. Earl Ferrers had an estate nearby,[5] and we know that Pickford visited Aston Lodge in 1762. Anne, the wife of Joseph Greaves of Aston Lodge, was the daughter of Sir Brooke Boothby of Ashbourne Hall, and half-sister to Brooke Boothby, the young friend of Dr Darwin. The Boothbys were the leading family in Ashbourne, and were familiar with, or related to, all the gentry in that area. They had lived at Ashbourne Hall since the seventeenth century, and over the years had turned a rambling, timber-framed house, into a large, dull, redbrick, classical structure, by facing up the exterior. When Boothby inherited his father's title in 1789, he spent some money on rebuilding and laying out the garden, but most of the house was demolished after the Second World War, leaving only one very dilapidated wing standing.[6] It is possible that Pickford worked there, though what evidence we have is inconclusive.

There are three houses in the town that can reasonably be attributed to Pickford: the Grey House, 61 Church Street, which he refronted for Brian Hodgson; the Mansion, which he remodelled for Dr Taylor; and Francis Beresford's house in the Compton, now Lloyd's Bank. The first two date from 1763–5, and Compton House, which is almost a replica of 44 Friar Gate in Derby, from a year or so later.

No accounts have survived for these buildings, but we do know that Pickford was working in Ashbourne in 1763. An item in the account book for the Derby Assembly Rooms reads: 'March 19th. Pd. John Harris's expenses going to the quarry and comeing to Ashbourn for me'.[7] The rest can be surmised from Dr Johnson's correspondence.

Dr Taylor's second wife ran away in 1763, and in May the following year Johnson wrote to congratulate him 'on the happy end of so vexatious an affair', suggesting he divert himself with 'the improvement of your estate or little schemes of building'. In July 1765 Johnson wrote again to his friend referring in the letter 'to all your building and feasting'.[8]

In a *Country Life* article in 1968 Arthur Oswald discussed the history of the Mansion in some detail.[9] He concluded that the Grey House and the Mansion facing it across Church Street were by the same architect. He assumed the Mansion was the earlier of the two, but in the light of the new evidence it would seem to be the other way around. The story told locally that Dr Taylor was put out of countenance by the handsome façade on the house across the road may be correct after all.

Brian Hodgson was neither an Ashbournian nor a gentleman. He was born in Stafford and made his fortune as a high-class innkeeper, first at The George in Stamford and later at The Old Hall Hotel in Buxton, where he came into contact with the fashionable society. Either innkeeping was a very lucrative trade or he acquired his wealth by other means, because apart from his property in Ashbourne he also owned several other estates. He retired to Ashbourne in the 1750s and bought the Grey House, which had been built a few years earlier by Francis Higginbotham.[10]

It was evidently Hodgson's intention to take the local gentry by storm, or at least to show them that he was no ordinary tradesman, because soon after he moved in he determined to refront his house in the grandest possible manner. On stylistic grounds there can be little doubt that Pickford was the architect, but there is one piece of circumstantial evidence that links his name with Hodgson's. In the subscription list for the Derby Assembly Rooms Hodgson was the only person connected with trade who was allowed to make a contribution to the building fund.[11] It has been suggested that this was because he had the contract for serving suppers at the assembly, and it now appears that he owned the building next to the Assembly Rooms from which the meals were served.[12] It is also of interest that his contribution was the only one Pickford collected in person.

The façade of the Grey House is one of a number Pickford designed using the same combination of windows in the central bay. Another is Ogston Hall, Derbyshire, for which his drawings of 1767 still survive.[13] The arrangement

The Grey House, Church Street, Ashbourne, Derbyshire

consists of a tripartite, pedimented doorway with a Venetian window above and a half round, or Diocletian window, at the second-floor level, all grouped under a pediment. The idea seems to go back to a design by Hawksmoor in 1717–20, for a new entrance to Worcester College, Oxford.[14] Henry Flitcroft used it at Stivichal Hall,[15] Warwickshire, in 1755, and it was also a favourite of the Hiorne brothers. They used the idea at Kyre Park, Worcestershire, a house they remodelled in 1753–6, which must have been well known to Pickford.

The plan form is similar to his own house in Derby, consisting of a square entrance hall with reception rooms either side and the staircase in a compartment offset at the rear, which suggests that he must have remodelled the interior as well. The coffered ceiling is similar in form to the one in St Helen's House in Derby, though the execution is inferior.

Although among the earliest of Pickford's executed designs, the Grey House has one of his most successful street façades. In particular, the canted bays each side of the front porch help to give depth to the elevation. In some ways these bays are an anomaly having more to do with Elizabethan architecture than the Palladian tradition, but it does demonstrate how architects like Pickford were swayed more by English usage than the original works of the Italian master. As far as we know this is the only occasion he used this device, though he proposed something similar for Keele Hall, in Staffordshire.[16] Faced in keuper sandstone from a local quarry,[17] the Grey House sits perfectly with the Elizabethan grammar school next to it, showing how buildings of different centuries can stand in harmony with each other.

James Boswell dined with Hodgson during his stay in Ashbourne in 1777, and noted that he had 'a handsome house nearly opposite to Dr Taylor's. But Mr Hodgson is not of his party', meaning that he was a Tory.[18] Whether or not this increased the rivalry between them we cannot say, but we do know that Dr Taylor and Dr Johnson, who was also a Tory, argued incessantly over politics. Brian Hodgson died in December 1781, at the age of seventy-three, and is commemorated by a monument in Ashbourne church which assures us that he was an 'honest man and a sincere Christian'. It is one of a group of memorial plaques which can be associated with Joseph Pickford and the Derby sculptor, George Moneypenny.

If Brian Hodgson made his fortune from honest trade, the same could not be said of the Revd John Taylor. The Anglican Church was then notorious for the numbers of absentee parsons in its ranks and Taylor was one of the worst, enjoying the income from a number of benefices in which he was non-resident. Boswell observed that although he enjoyed an income of £1,000 a year from the Church alone 'he does very little duty, but resides almost constantly at his house . . . in Ashbourne, that he may keep up a political interest in the place, to be of consequence to the Devonshire family, in hopes of higher preferment'.[19] Taylor had a love of good living and ostentatious display as

Hester Thrale noticed during her visit in 1774. She remarked on 'the elegance and splendour of Dr Taylor's surroundings at Ashbourne; his fine pictures which he does not understand . . . a glorious harpsichord which he sends for a young man out of town to play upon, a waterfall running at the foot of his garden, deer in his paddock . . . his table liberally spread, his wines all excellent of their kind . . . '. It is little wonder he was known as 'the King of Ashbourne'.[20]

The Mansion before Dr Taylor began to remodel it was a typical seventeenth-century, gabled house, H-shaped with the open ends facing the garden and the road. The work was done in two or three phases; first he refronted the street façade, next he added an octagon room at the rear and finally he demolished most of the interior at the front of the house to form a large entrance hall carried up through two storeys.

If Dr Taylor had hoped that the new front to his house would rival that of Brian Hodgson's, he must have been greatly disappointed. Although superficially the same, they do not really compare in quality. The redbrick façade of the Mansion is much inferior in quality and suffers from being in almost permanent shade. However, it does have one feature of interest, the brick voussoir frieze in the pediment. Pickford must have approved of it as he used it again on his own house in Derby.

The Mansion, Church Street, Ashbourne, Derbyshire

Perhaps Dr Taylor himself regretted the street façade, because when he came to build the octagon, he chose the same keuper sandstone that Brian Hodgson had used. The dating of this room can be fixed with certainty as Dr Johnson refers to it in a letter of 15 July 1765: 'Let me know', he wrote, 'how you go on in the world and what entertainments may be expected in your new room.'[21] It was in this same octagon in September 1777 that Boswell proposed to celebrate Dr Johnson's birthday by lighting the chandelier, but Johnson forbade it, having, as he said, a 'horror' of such occasions and 'would not have the lustre lit on his account'.[22]

The octagon room was an elegant solution to a difficult problem. The form chosen fits perfectly between the wings of the old house, the part seen from the garden forming a canted bay, with a pedimented door in the centre and steps down to the garden. The general proportions are excellent, both inside and out, with good quality rococo plasterwork in the domed ceiling. Like the Grey House it has the advantage of sitting in the sunlight, which gives it that sculptured look which all architects like.

The alterations to the staircase and entrance hall can also be dated with certainty as the work was in progress during Dr Johnson's last visit to Ashbourne in 1784, two years after Pickford's death. Johnson was not at all

The Octagon Room, The Mansion, Ashbourne

Interior of the mansion, Church Street,
Ashbourne

happy, and wondered what had impelled his old friend to make such drastic
alterations to his house at his time of life. We may wonder too, as the weak
neo-classical design is so inferior to the earlier work. Again the architect can
only be guessed at, but Pickford's old assistant, Thomas Gardner, would seem
to be a likely candidate.

Three miles north of Ashbourne, on the limestone plateau, stands the home
of the FitzHerbert family, Tissington Hall, one of the most picturesque seats in
the county. The original Jacobean house overlooking the village is backed by
an eighteenth-century range facing the garden. No accounts have survived to
confirm Pickford's claim, but William FitzHerbert (1712–72) knew him well
and there can be little doubt that the design was his.

FitzHerbert was a leading figure in local society and well known in London
circles. John Wilkes wrote to him with affection, and as a Member of
Parliament for Derby from 1762, he supported the radical cause in the
company of the Duke of Devonshire and his party.[23] Like Pickford he was a
Freemason and a member of a London lodge, which suggests a common
meeting ground, though this cannot be confirmed. He saw himself as being 'as
independent a man as any in the House', an assessment which was generally
accepted by his political opponents as well as his friends.[24] Lord Hyde said of
him:

There are few men I would sooner oblige than FitzHerbert. His parts, his knowledge, his humanity, and utility make the foundation of my esteem. I might add his moderation notwithstanding his warmth for Wilkes which I believe was kindled by the coolness of others in seeing that unhappy man in jeopardy. I know few second rate men that could be better employed by one in power.[25]

Dr Johnson, who knew FitzHerbert well, left the best description of him:

There was no sparkle, no brilliancy about him, but I never knew a man who was so generally acceptable. He made everybody quite easy, overpowered nobody by superiority of his talents, made no man think worse of himself by being his rival, seemed always to listen, did not oblige you to hear much from him, and did not oppose what you said. Everybody liked him, but he had no friend, as I understand the word, nobody with whom he exchanged intimate thoughts.[26]

As a man who could command the respect of both Wilkes and Johnson he must have been the personification of tact and an ideal magistrate. Yet in the end he took his own life in tragic circumstances. Walpole described how it happened:

He went to see the convicts executed that morning and from thence, in his boots, to his son, having sent his groom out of the way. At three, his son said, 'Sir, you are to dine at Mr Buller's, it is time for you to go home and dress.' He went to his own stable and hanged himself with a bridle. They say his circumstances were in great disorder.[27]

But Dr Johnson, who was no stranger to melancholy, thought otherwise. He was of the opinion that his suicide 'was owing to imaginary difficulties in his affairs, which, had he talked with a friend, would soon have vanished'.[28] FitzHerbert's place in the House of Commons was taken by another of Pickford's Derbyshire patrons, Wenman Coke of Longford Hall.

The building history of Tissington Hall is not easy to unravel. William FitzHerbert inherited the estate from his father in 1739, but did nothing to the house for nearly twenty years. Perhaps he preferred to live at Old St Helen's in Derby, another family property, which would have been more convenient for him to discharge his duties as Recorder.[29] His mother, a Bagshawe heiress, lived on until 1762. After her death he inherited Bagshawe Hall at Bakewell and other property, the sale of which may have provided the cash to carry out the major building works at Tissington. Certainly the date was about right.

During his mother's lifetime he did remodel the Jacobean entrance hall in a pretty rococo Gothick style, which is the only part of his improvements we can date with certainty. A bill for the Gothick chimney-piece survives, dated 13 June 1757, and shows that 'Daniel Sephton and Henry Watson, measured and valued' the work at £54 2s. 5d.[30] As it is highly unlikely they would value their own work, the carver may have been Joseph Hall of Derby, as an item in the account refers to 'carriage and boxes by Mr Hall's bill'. If he was the carver, what part did Sephton and Watson play in the matter? Henry Watson was a well-known Derbyshire carver, but as Sephton's name heads the account he must have been the principal.

Daniel Sephton was the son of Henry Sephton of Liverpool (1686–1756) a master builder and architect who designed Ince Blundell Hall and a number of other important buildings in the city. Henry Sephton was buried at Walton near Liverpool, where a tablet, destroyed by bombing in the Second World War, also commemorated his wife Esther and his son Daniel, 'late of Manchester, Eminent in Carving', who died on 11 January 1759, aged forty-five.[31]

An explanation could be that Daniel, like his father, also practiced as an architect and was responsible for the overall design of the room, though we now know that the design of the chimney-piece itself was taken from Batty Langley's book. If this was the case then Henry Watson would have been

Tissington Hall, Tissington, Derbyshire

Tissington Hall, Tissington, Derbyshire

acting as his local agent. It is worth noting that the chimney-piece, the hall paving, and the three lancet windows that look out on to the garden, were all carved from Hopton Wood stone, suggesting that the work was conceived by one man.

The second phase of FitzHerbert's work, the three-storey block facing the garden, was added a few years later. Though placed directly behind the hall, it is clearly not by the same hand. This addition can be firmly attributed to Joseph Pickford.

At first sight the six-bay front is very gauche, but the architect cleverly disguises this unfortunate solecism with a central canted bay projecting through the two lower storeys. Externally this gives the appearance of a five-bay façade restoring uniformity to the building. This type of bay was a feature of Lansdowne House, Berkeley Square, begun about 1762 by Robert Adam for the Earl of Bute, a building which Pickford knew well. The same idea was used at Wanlip Hall near Leicester, which can also be attributed to the Derby architect. This suggests that the garden front at Tissington was added about 1765.

The entire ground floor is taken up by a loggia, open to the garden on one side, similar, though not identical, to the loggia on Pickford's own house in

Derby. Today this area is very dank and unattractive and the rear wall through which one would ideally pass to the hall behind contains only the three windows described above. Perhaps these were left this way because of the awkward change of level between the loggia and the hall, though any passage between the two would have been unhappy, as the robust order of the loggia has nothing in common with the delicate Gothic plasterwork inside the hall.

Above the loggia are three reception rooms, and on the second floor family or servants' bedrooms. Extensive alterations early this century have greatly changed the appearance of these rooms, and very little is left of the original work except an impressive chimney-piece in the central drawing room with the projecting bay. This is typical of Pickford's work and like so many of his fire surrounds is carved out of white Carrara marble with Siena inset panels, reminiscent of work in his own house.

The stone used in the building is all local. The infill walling is carboniferous limestone, probably from a quarry on the estate. The window surrounds and architectural embellishments are in keuper sandstone from Stanton, north of Ashbourne on the Leek road, the quarry that provided the stone for the twelfth-century tower of Thorpe church, but more importantly for this study for the houses in Ashbourne which we attribute to Joseph Pickford.[32]

FitzHerbert had at least three houses in which we know he lived: Tissington Hall, Old St Helen's in Derby, and his London house in Queen Street, Marylebone, where he seems to have enjoyed a most convivial life. We know of his Masonic activities and John Wilkes talked about 'our convivial friends in the Beef Steak Club'.[33] These were probably his Parliamentary colleagues, and others of the same background and political persuasion.

He had business connections or was friendly with a number of Pickford's clients including John Gisborne of St Helen's House in Derby, who wrote the son a touching letter after his father's death. Perhaps it was this close association that persuaded FitzHerbert to purchase a plot of land on Nun's Green as part of the Friar Gate development that Pickford was planning. It is not clear from the deeds which of Pickford's plots was described as 'lying westward to the ground purchased by William FitzHerbert Esquire', but evidently FitzHerbert did not build on it himself.[34]

Closely related to the FitzHerberts were the Meynells of Bradley Hall, some three miles to the east of Ashbourne, a curious place with an unusual history. The house was adapted in the early 1770s by Hugo Meynell (1735–1808) from a stable block of some size, which he had built earlier to accommodate his hunters and pack.

This building was conceived as part of a larger scheme to replace the old moated, timber-framed house, which has now completely disappeared, though the moat can still be seen in the field nearby. However, on second thoughts, Hugo moved to Hoar Cross Hall, Staffordshire, and converted his stables into a lodge which he seldom used 'except for the convenience of hunting in the neighbourhood'.[35] This change of heart may have been brought about by his election as MP for Lichfield.

The Meynells were well known to Dr Johnson, especially the father, Littleton Poyntz Meynell (died 1753), who carried irascible eccentricity to the point of madness. But if certain of the male members of the family were best avoided, that could not be said of the women, in particular Hugo's sister Mary, who married William FitzHerbert of Tissington Hall.

According to Johnson, 'she had the best understanding I ever met with in any human being', and moreover, 'she would have been handsome for a queen: her beauty had more in it of majesty than of attraction, more of the dignity of virtue than the vivacity of wit.' However, after marriage he somewhat modified his opinion. Now he found 'her first care was to preserve her husband's soul from corruption; her second, to keep his estate entire for their children. . . . She stood at the door of her Paradise in Derbyshire, like the angel with the flaming sword, to keep the devil at a distance.'[36]

Today, the interior of Bradley Hall is very much as Hugo Meynell left it. Externally the house is a hotch-potch, but inside all is of a piece. There are no records to show that Pickford was the architect, but the work is all in his style, and it is almost inconceivable to think there was another builder in the district who possessed his design flair. It is for this reason that the work is attributed to him.

The interior is far from plain, boasting a most impressive staircase hall, which suggests the house was designed with entertainment in mind. The staircase itself is of timber, with three turned balusters per tread and carved tread-ends.

The hall is separated from the dining room by a pedimented door surround, and the dining room itself has a large bay taking up the entire end wall; octagonal outside, but reduced to a curve in the interior. The fine plasterwork is all in keeping with the rest of the design; the ceiling in the dining room is coffered very much after the style of St Helen's House in Derby and other work by Pickford.

Like the Meynells, the Beresfords were also near neighbours of the FitzHerberts. They had estates around Dove Dale and a family seat at Fenny Bentley which they abandoned to a tenant in favour of a more comfortable house in Ashbourne. The house in Ashbourne came into the family when John Beresford (1687–1755) married the daughter of John FitzHerbert of Somersal Herbert, a collateral branch of the Tissington FitzHerberts. Their eldest son Richard (1731–90) inherited the property in Ashbourne, leaving the younger, more dynamic brother, Francis, to provide for himself.

Francis Beresford (1737–1801) was trained as an attorney, but made his fortune as an industrial entrepreneur. He had interests in coal mining and the

Butterley Company, which by the end of the century was one of the largest producers of iron in the country. He was also one of the promoters of the Cromford Canal, which connected Arkwright's mill village at Cromford with Butterley and Nottingham.[37]

He moved back to Ashbourne from Nottingham in the early 1760s, and lived for a while in Dove House behind the Market Place before moving to his new house on the Compton. There are no early deeds for Compton House, but an abstract of title refers to a release of land in the Compton to Francis in 1765.[38] He was then twenty-eight years old and about to marry Fanny Reynolds of Chesterfield, so 1765–7 seems to be the most likely building date, a year or two before the house in Friar Gate.

Nicolson tells us that between 1762 and 1765 Wright painted a portrait of a 'Mr Beresford'. This he assumes to be Francis as he had business connections with Wright. Perhaps it was done in anticipation of the marriage and the new house.

Compton House is one of the most impressive of Pickford's smaller designs. Certainly the quality of the stonework and the detailing leaves nothing to be desired, which makes one wonder why the front façade was placed directly on to the pavement. Unlike Dr Taylor and Brian Hodgson, Beresford was not

The Beresford house, The Compton, Ashbourne, Derbyshire

limited by the constraints of an existing building. Had he wished he could have set it back behind a carriage sweep to match his impressive gardens at the rear. This seems to be such an obvious thing to do that there must have been some reason unknown to us which limited his course of action.

Like Pickford on his own house, Beresford chose to concentrate the expense and show on the street façade. At the rear the garden front was redbrick and penny plain without any pretensions whatsoever. In comparison with 44 Friar Gate the chief interest lies in the different use of brick and stone. In design the differences are slight but significant. At Ashbourne there is a heavy modillion cornice below the attic storey, whereas in Friar Gate the cornice is above, giving a different emphasis to the windows on the second floor. Apart from that the stone gives more dignity and weight. The stone window surrounds set in the brickwork at Friar Gate seem slight by comparison.

There are no known contemporary descriptions of the house, but it seemed to suit Francis and his wife Fanny who lived to bring twelve children into the world. Francis died on 18 November 1801 and is commemorated by a handsome plaque in Fenny Bentley church carved by Joseph Hall of Derby. Buried with him is his wife Fanny who died in 1815, and nine of his children.

The Beresford family lived at Compton House until 1840 when it was purchased by the Burton Old Bank. At this date, or shortly afterwards, it was divided into two, as it is today. Half the premises were reserved for banking transactions, and half for the manager's house. None of the original features have survived in the bank, but the manager's house has fared better. There we can still see the staircase and fireplace in Hopton Wood stone. The design of the fireplace is typical Pickford, with glyphs in the frieze and rosettes in the pilasters. It is very similar to the one in the hall at St Helen's House in Derby and of the same date.

CHAPTER SEVEN

St Helen's House, Derby

For an English gentleman, architect or painter, to undertake a journey to Italy in the eighteenth century in order to complete his education was so commonplace as scarcely to merit comment. But for an Italian architect to visit England was indeed a curiosity, even more so when his travels brought him into Derbyshire. But such was the case with Gianantonio Selva (1751–1819).[1]

Selva, a native of the city of Venice, was well grounded in the arts. He had been a pupil of the architect Tommaso Temanza, the founder of the Venetian Academy, as well as studying painting under Antonio Visentini. Temanza was the leading neo-Palladian of his day and taught Selva well, which gave him a solid foundation for his own architectural career. Selva's work included a number of villas and churches in Venice, but he is best remembered today for the Teatro della Fenice, subsequently the scene of many of Verdi's greatest triumphs.

His manuscript diary of the journey, now in the Querini-Stampalia Library in Venice, shows that he arrived in England in June 1781, and departed again for the continent at the beginning of September. He entered Derbyshire from the north towards the end of July and arrived in Derby on 1 August. Of Derby he says, 'Here are some buildings of substantial architecture, in particular at the entrance to the city coming from Chesterfield there is a house near the New Inn with a circular courtyard of much merit. The architect of it was Mr Pickford and although he was never in Italy he is one of the best of my acquaintance.'[2]

In spite of the hint of condescension in his tone there is no doubting his sincerity and appreciation of Pickford's work. The New Inn, to which he refers, formerly stood at the top of Bridge Gate, on the opposite corner to St Helen's House. In front of St Helen's part of the wall that formed the semi-circular courtyard is still standing, and early maps of the town and engravings of the house show the wall complete.

Clearly Selva was no ordinary traveller.[3] During his stay in London, the Venetian ambassador showed him around and introduced him to well-connected connoisseurs. He visited most of the buildings of interest in the capital, but had little good to say of English architects or architecture, which makes his warm appreciation of Pickford even more surprising. It is true that St Helen's House is one of the better Palladian buildings of provincial England, but it does not compare with the Horse Guards which Selva held in very low regard. Perhaps it was Pickford's personality that impressed him, as he had forgotten the name of the only other English architect he met.

It was not by chance that Selva called on Pickford. Clearly he had an introduction, but who was it that brought them together? We know that Selva had an interest in science and dined with members of the Royal Society. John Whitehurst was living in London by 1781, and though Selva does not mention him by name, it is possible he was present at that dinner. Selva certainly met Joseph Priestley, who was a member of the Lunar Society, and later, on his journey north, he called on Matthew Boulton and visited his Soho Works.[4]

Although these are only matters for speculation, we now know, thanks to Selva, that Joseph Pickford was the architect of one of the most impressive town houses in the midland counties. If he had been responsible for no other building that alone would have established his reputation as an architect.

John Gisborne (1716–79), the builder of St Helen's House, was a member of a family of gentrified businessmen who claimed to have originated in Hartington, but had lived in Derby for several generations. The first to reach prominence was elected mayor of Derby in 1659. After that they continued to build their fortune and with it their political power. In 1774 John Gisborne was returned to Parliament for the Borough of Derby in the Whig interest, but was later unseated after an enquiry found his methods of electioneering too much to stomach, even for those unruly times. By contrast, his son Thomas was a cultivated radical, a friend of Wilberforce, and an intimate friend and pupil of Joseph Wright.[5]

None of the Gisborne family archives has survived, but St Helen's can be dated with some certainty by the correspondence of Josiah Wedgwood. John Gisborne was an old friend of Wedgwood's and was partly responsible for introducing him to Pickford, a meeting that led to the building of Etruria Hall.

In December 1767 Wedgwood wrote to his partner Thomas Bentley: 'I was only one night at Derby, and lay at Mr Gisborne's whose new house pleases me much, but not entirely.'[6] Taken in conjunction with two advertisements in the *Derby Mercury*, the first dated 29 May 1767, seeking a tenant 'for a large convenient house in Bridge Gate . . . in the possession of Mr John Gisborne . . . enquiries to Joseph Pickford on Nun's Green', and a second of 16 October, where the same property is described as 'late in the possession of Mr John Gisborne', it seems reasonable to suppose that the new house was complete by the summer of 1767.

Externally St Helen's House is a plain, redbrick box, with no

Lansdowne House, Berkeley Square, London

embellishments save for the fine ashlar façade facing King Street, which Selva so greatly admired. The inspiration for this design came from an unusual source. About five years earlier Robert Adam had designed a new London town house for the Earl of Bute in Berkeley Square.[7] Before the house was finished he sold it to John FitzMaurice 1st Marquess of Lansdowne, a condition of the sale being that the house should be completed by Adam at Lord Bute's expense. The house was finally finished in 1768.

The principal façade must have been completed some years earlier because it is virtually identical in form and proportion to St Helen's House. The only variations are in the detail. Whereas Adam worked in his newer neo-classical style with plain surfaces, Pickford deliberately looks back to the time of William Kent, with window surrounds and other Palladian embellishments. In particular with the Ionic capitals, Pickford uses the traditional Italianate form whereas Adam, with his greater understanding of recent archaeology, looks back to its Grecian predecessor.

Adam's design for Lansdowne House was not published until 1773[8], so it must have been the building itself that Pickford studied. It is possible that Pickford knew Lord Lansdowne and was given access to the house while it was under construction. Lansdowne was a patron of the sciences, and was well known to members of the Lunar Society. He gave Dr Priestley accommodation at Bowood and his London house,[9] and it is known that John Whitehurst made him a pair of wheel barometers.[10]

As Pickford designed St Helen's, the house was flanked by two semi-circular walls topped with ball finials after the manner of Inigo Jones. The front to King Street was closed off with pedimented, arched gateway piers joined by a wrought-

Engraving of St Helen's House, Derby

iron fence. As far as we know this was removed when the road was widened in the 1870s. By this date the house had become the home of the Derby Grammar School and the gateways may have been acquired by one of the governors, Charles Arkwright. At that time he lived at Spondon Field House, which is now the site of a comprehensive school. But the entrance to the old park is still adorned by two fine Palladian piers, similar, but not identical to those at St Helen's. It is probable that they are one and the same, re-erected in a truncated form.[11]

The plan of St Helen's is typical of Pickford's town houses; it is somewhat like the Hodgson House in Ashbourne, or his own house in Friar Gate. The principal rooms are on the ground floor and open off a central hall. The staircase is in a separate compartment at the rear, but unlike Pickford's own house there is no wall between the entrance hall and the staircase so that the magnificent wrought-iron balustrade to the staircase can clearly be seen by the visitor as he enters the house.

This balustrade was the work of Benjamin Yates, the former apprentice and foreman of the celebrated Derby smith, Robert Bakewell, who died in 1752. After his master's death Yates set up a new workshop in the Wardwick,[12] by St Werburgh's church, where he continued to turn out Bakewell's old designs. The balustrade had been used by Bakewell, first at the Maister's House in Hull, and later at Okeover Hall. Yates had used it at the Nuthall Temple and later at Earl Ferrers' house, Staunton Harold. We know that Ferrers was a friend of Gisborne and possibly proposed the design to him. Yates lived on until 1776 and almost certainly worked with Pickford elsewhere, as we know he supplied tools to him when he was supervising the workmen at Foremark Hall.[13]

The other room of distinction, the library, formerly the dining room, opens off the entrance hall on the left-hand side. It has a fine rococo ceiling, with the plasterwork featuring a trailing vine. It is tempting to attribute this work to Abraham Denstone, the talented Derby plasterer who was then working at Kedleston, but it is more likely to be the work of another man employed directly by

St Helen's House, Derby

Pickford. A year or so later Josiah Wedgwood wrote to his partner Thomas Bentley to say that Pickford was prepared to lend to them his plasterer, who was skilled at modelling in miniature, to teach their young apprentices.[14] In the end he did not go over to Etruria, which is a pity, for if he had we might have learned his name.

In the dining room there is a particularly fine chimney-piece in Carrara and Siena marble, its exuberance contrasting with the more sober Doric piece in the hall, carved out of homely Hopton Wood stone. At the east end of the dining room there is a large depressed arch, which once contained a double door leading to the drawing room, but is now blocked off. The entire suite of rooms on the ground floor originally opened off the entrance hall and staircase, no doubt better to facilitate the pleasures of the Derby Rout and other convivial entertainments.

William Hutton, the Derby historian, writing in 1791 for once has something good to say about a building designed by Pickford, but as always there is a sting in the tail. Of St Helen's he writes:

But the most superb [house] is that of John Gisborne, Esq., in Bridge Gate, a house that would honour the first orders of Nobility, but in a situation that would not merit a dwelling of £500. Where ever we find so expensive a work, we may fairly conclude the proprietor was very rich, or did not dread poverty.[15]

In this he has a point, as any prudent observer would ask, why build such a fine house in such a cramped position at the corner of Bridge Gate, with a whole park to chose from? The explanation seems to be that Gisborne was not able to acquire the land to form the park until some years after the house was completed.[16]

Before 1756 the Sheffield turnpike had followed the line of what is now Darley Grove, between St Helen's House and the River Derwent. With this removed the possibilities for the park were greatly improved, and though no records have survived the final layout was almost certainly the work of Pickford's old associate, William Emes (1729–1804).[17] The park did not reach its full maturity until after the Gisborne family had sold out to William Strutt, but in 1819 North Parade off Bridge Gate was set out and the new housing development destroyed the rural tranquillity of the place for ever. By the turn of the century the whole area had been covered with housing, and all that remains today is the name Strutt's Park.

The house now numbered 11 to 16 Bridge Gate, where Gisborne lived before he moved into St Helen's House in 1767, has today been changed out of all recognition, but a handsome Doric entrance porch, almost certainly by Pickford, still survives, but not in its original position. As there is no documentary evidence we cannot determine who was responsible for this work. It may have been Gisborne himself, but more probably it was the Curzon family who purchased the house from him.

It passed from the Curzons by marriage to the Beaumonts of Barrow upon Trent, who in turn gave it to the Catholic church who incorporated it into the present convent building in the 1840s, after Pugin had erected St Mary's church next door.[18] Originally the Doric porch faced west, but has now been turned through ninety degrees to face south. The hall, which opened off the porch, is now isolated within the body of the convent building, and it is no longer possible to see the full extent of Pickford's alterations.

Pickford's connection with another house of almost identical design to St Helen's is confirmed by the correspondence of Josiah Wedgwood. In September 1768 Wedgwood suggested to his partner Thomas Bentley that he might contact Pickford at 'The Hams near Coleshill', a house for which no documentation has survived.[19]

According to Burke's *Visitation of Seats*, Hams Hall, Warwickshire, was built by C.B. Adderley in 1764, though another authority gives the date as 1760. If 1760 is correct Adderley commenced his undertaking at the tender age of seventeen. Logic suggests the later date, as in that year he came of age.

Charles Bowyer Adderley was a member of an old Staffordshire family with Derbyshire estates at Thorpe and Snitterton near Ashbourne where Pickford was already working. His father's first wife was a Horton of Catton Hall, which was designed by William Smith and built under the supervision of Pickford's father or uncle.[20] In 1774 Pickford himself rebuilt the steeple of Solihull church,[21] a contract

Hams Hall, Warwickshire

which may have come through the Adderley family. These are all pointers which help Pickford's case, but it is doubtful now if the final proof will ever be discovered.

St Helen's House and Hams Hall must have been commissioned about the same time, so it is difficult to say which was designed first. Both houses are ashlar-faced, seven-bays wide, with the three central bays grouped under a pediment with Ionic pilasters carried through the two upper storeys. The differences are slight: St Helen's has the ground floor windows set in arched recesses, whereas at Hams Hall the wall is plain. St Helen's is certainly more stylish and richer in detail, but there is no difficulty in attributing the two buildings to the same architect.

Hams Hall was demolished about 1920, when the upper part of the façade was taken to Gloucestershire and rebuilt, along with its interior fittings, at Bledisloe Lodge. The proportions and character of what remains of the building have completely changed. Only the top two storeys were rebuilt with the original ground-floor windows built into the second floor.[22] We should be grateful that any of it was saved, but if the architect were to return today, it is doubtful he would recognize his own offspring.

CHAPTER EIGHT

Etruria Hall

It was during the autumn of 1767 that Pickford first became acquainted with
the celebrated potter, Josiah Wedgwood (1730–95). Their mutual friend,
John Whitehurst, knew that Wedgwood was looking for an architect and the
introduction almost certainly came through him. Their first meeting was a
great success. 'I like the Man,' Wedgwood told his partner Thomas Bentley,
'and think to agree with him to do all my work, as that method will save me a
deal of trouble.'[1] Little did he realize how much trouble he would have before
the contract was complete.

Josiah Wedgwood, then thirty-seven years of age, had already achieved a
national reputation for his Queen's Ware, named in honour of Queen
Charlotte, who in turn had granted him the title, Potter to Her Majesty. With
such patronage to boost his business it was not long before Wedgwood's
pottery adorned the tables of the wealthy throughout Europe.[2]

Wedgwood knew what he wanted, nothing less than a new town devoted to
the manufacture of his pottery, with a grand house for himself, another for his
partner, a pottery works and houses for his workers. At the suggestion of
Erasmus Darwin, he gave it the name of Etruria, in the mistaken belief that
the pottery he intended to make there was Etruscan.[3] Though he chose a
romantic name he was in no doubt about what it would all cost. Pickford, on
the other hand, seldom seemed to get his estimates right, which to a
businessman like Wedgwood was a source of great irritation.

The situation he chose for his new town was far from promising. In July
1766 he purchased 350 acres of land between Hanley and Newcastle, known
as the Ridge House Estate. It was a barren moor with no protection from the
weather, about as far removed from his idealized Etruria as it was possible to
be, but it did have one advantage. Since 1764 Wedgwood and Bentley had
been involved with a project for cutting a navigation between the River Trent
and the Mersey, known as the Grand Trunk Scheme. The Grand Trunk Bill
received royal assent in May 1766, two months before Wedgwood completed
his purchase. Though altruism played a large part in Wedgwood's involvement
with the canal, he was also aware, because of his friendship with James

Brindley, the canal engineer, that the navigation would pass close by the Ridge House Estate, at a point where he intended to place his new pottery works.[4]

Before the canal was cut the local potters carried their wares out by packhorse, a costly means of transport because of the many breakages they suffered on the rough Staffordshire roads. The canal longboat solved the problem, but in this matter, as in most of his entrepreneurial activities, Wedgwood was well ahead of his rivals.

The new potworks was to be at the heart of the town, standing by the canal alongside the turnpike road between Hanley and Newcastle. To the north-east, on rising ground, and masked from the works by a plantation, Wedgwood sited his new house, Etruria Hall. Also in the park, but over by the turnpike, he positioned Bank House, for his partner Thomas Bentley. The houses for the workers, forty-two in number, he situated to the west of the works on low-lying land between the canal and Foulea Brook.[5] All of these contracts he entrusted to Pickford who was engaged at Etruria for the next four years.

For advice on building Wedgwood looked first to his friends and fellow members of the Lunar Society, John Whitehurst and Erasmus Darwin. Darwin was the greatest polymath of his day, and though he was later surpassed in reputation by his grandson, he is still remembered as a physician, poet, philosopher, inventor and, in spite of a stammer, as a wit and raconteur. Coleridge, the poet, visited him and wrote:

> Derby is full of curiosities, the cotton, the silk mills, Wright the painter and Dr Darwin the everything except the Christian. Dr Darwin possesses perhaps a greater range of knowledge than any other person in Europe, and is the most inventive of philosophical men. He thinks in a new train on all . . .[6]

That is clearly what Wedgwood thought as well, as he consulted his friend about most things. Pickford certainly knew Darwin, and there was at least one meeting in Lichfield between Wedgwood, Darwin and Pickford, to discuss estimates and to examine 'a model of a windmill of Dr Darwin's projection'.[7] This curiosity, which later appears on early engravings of Etruria, was used for grinding the raw materials in the process of making pottery.

In his correspondence with Thomas Bentley, the earliest reference Wedgwood makes to building at Etruria was in July 1767, when he tells his partner, 'our friend Whitehurst is coming over to discuss our business'.[8] Nothing further is said until the end of November when Wedgwood went to Derby himself, 'finally to settle the plan with Mr Whitehurst and Mr Pickford'.[9] A few days later he returned full of enthusiasm for his new architect: 'Mr Whitehurst was away from home, but Mr Pickford and I soon settled our plan and have made it 140 sq. ft. less than we chalked out here when Mr Whitehurst was with us.'[10]

Thomas Bentley by Joseph Wright

Of all the building that was done by Pickford at Etruria only Etruria Hall is still standing today, and that in a very mutilated form. Bank House survived for about fifty years and was demolished in the early nineteenth century before an illustration was made of it. In a sense Bank House was doomed before it was built. Bentley was a sophisticated cosmopolitan who only agreed to come to the Potteries under great pressure from his partner. Rural life was not for him. He finally moved from Liverpool to London to manage the sales and distribution and never occupied Bank House himself, though Wedgwood lived there for a time until his own house was finished.

The discussions between Wedgwood, Bentley and their architect were quickly resolved, as by the end of January 1768 the plans were finalized. Wedgwood sided with Pickford, and Bentley's ideas for his own house were curtly pushed aside.

The enclosed [plan] is laid before you for your approbation as Mr Pickford has many objections to that you sent him. The chimneys can not be made tolerable, nor the elevation, nor many other things, and he says this will be built as cheap as the other not withstanding the stonework and the elegance of the elevation. The brew house and stables may be added in several ways if you approve of the rest. . . . We have now settled my plan for the house and works and Mr Pickford takes them away with him to make the estimates.[11]

The estimates came a few weeks later as on 3 March Wedgwood was in a more philosophical mood:

This building of houses, my friend, as far as we have hitherto gone is akin to building castles in the air. The old mansions are all swept away and you see a totally new one in their stead. Survey and admire this last and perfect work of your friend, but do not presume to alter a line or angle in the whole fabric, for I have sworn not to waver any longer so help me. . . . This plan [for Etruria Hall] will be executed for £500 or £700 less than the former, it is more in the modern taste, and much better adapted for the situation. On Thursday next [at Dr Darwin's] I am to meet Mr Pickford at Lichfield on my way to London, when we are finally to conclude everything respecting the building. . . . He had not made your estimate when we met, but said £400 was the least it [Bank House] would cost. I told him to reduce the expense to £350 without altering the dimensions.[12]

Upon this basis work on all three buildings now began. Pickford was not in attendance himself, the direction of the works he entrusted to his assistant,

Thomas Gardner. The foreman at Etruria Hall was 'Mr Eglington'. This was probably Samuel Eglington who saw the job out, as his brother Benjamin, the foreman at the Derby Assembly Rooms, died in 1768.[13]

The year 1768 was not a good one for Josiah Wedgwood either. Apart from his business worries, he also had to face up to the most traumatic experience of his life. For many years Wedgwood had suffered great agony with his knee. Finally in desperation Dr Darwin consulted James Bent, a Newcastle surgeon, and together they decided the best course of action was to take his leg off. The amputation took place at Wedgwood's house on 31 May 1768, a date he later called 'St Amputation Day'. Refusing to have the operation hidden from his view he sat upright in his chair while the two surgeons did their work.[14]

To return to more mundane matters, by the beginning of July Etruria Hall and Bank House were up to plinth height. Then on 8 September the bombshell struck. In a state of some alarm Wedgwood wrote to his partner:

I have enclosed Mr Pickford's new estimate for your house amounting – I dare not tell you all at once and therefore have not cast up the several long columns of figures. . . . I am much displeased with Mr Pickford and have stopped his men going on with your house.[15]

A week later Wedgwood wrote again:

. . . the contents were an estimate of your house by Mr Pickford and his clerk amounting to upwards of £800 . . . Mr Pickford came and stayed here until Monday afternoon. I talked to him a good deal about the two estimates and told him the difference betwixt them was the most extraordinary thing of that kind I had ever known . . . He acknowledged he had been guilty of an error, was sorry for it and would do everything in his power to make the house agreeable to us both. He would make a present of the surveying and desire only to be paid barely what it cost him. I told him I could give no further answer (till you came over).[16]

As the estimate for Bank House was not discussed again and work restarted after a short delay we must assume that Bentley saw Pickford face to face and worked out an agreeable compromise. Bank House was covered in for the winter, but was not finished until June 1769, when Wedgwood and his family moved in until his own house was finished a year later in September 1770.[17]

Of Bank House we can say very little, as it was demolished in 1819[18] and there is no known illustration of it. We know from Pickford's letter that it was to be 'as cheap as the other not withstanding the stonework and the elegance of the elevation',[19] which suggests that the main façade at least was of brick with stone dressings. In all probability it was similar in appearance to Etruria

Hall, but on a more modest scale, beyond that we would not wish to hazard a guess.

Etruria Hall in its heyday was in every respect a gentleman's residence, though its situation must have been very bleak indeed until Wedgwood's planting began to show through. This was not the work of Capability Brown as Eliza Meteyard suggests, but William Emes, Pickford's old comrade in arms.[20] Meteyard was writing in the 1860s when the park still existed, and though she speaks of it with affection, the illustration she gives of the house viewed from the lake must have been selected with some care to avoid the sight of encroaching industry.

The house as constructed was five bays wide and three storeys high. It was an elegant, redbrick box, with a double pile, slated roof behind a stone entablature relieved with ball finials. The main façade was conventional, with the three central bays stepped forward and grouped under a pediment. The rear elevation was more original. This was a variation of the main front of Ogston Hall which was built at the same time. This again was of five bays with the central bay containing the entrance door recessed. The side elevations were blocked off with the wings constructed during Wedgwood's lifetime, but from early engravings we know these had central Venetian windows echoing the semi-circular arches in the corridor, which still runs the full width of the building.

Inside nothing has survived from Pickford's time except a simple Chinese style balustrade to the servants' staircase, though it is rumoured that some of the original plasterwork still exists behind the modern suspended ceiling. After the Wedgwoods sold out and moved to Barlaston, the house became the offices of the Shelton Iron Company. It was under Shelton's regime that the building sunk to its present state of disrepair.

In spite of all the vexations Wedgwood suffered from his architect, the house, when completed, was well received. Dr Darwin reported that Captain Keir, another member of the Lunar Society, 'admires the plan of your house, and says it is fit for a prince'.[21] Eliza Metyard, who knew the house before it was despoiled, wrote of it: 'The principal rooms, opening from a hall which ran the whole length of the house, were large, well proportioned and lofty. The windows and staircase were ample; and capacity existed everywhere for decorative effects. . . .'[22] Although he did not realize it at the time Wedgwood was about to set a fashion among his fellow potters for the Palladian mansion.

There are several contemporary descriptions of Etruria, but for an unbiased report we shall content ourselves by quoting Lord Torrington who passed that way in 1792:

Now I enquired for Etruria, the grand pottery establish'd by Mr Wedgwood; and putting up my horses at the adjacent inn, sent up my

Etruria Hall, Etruria, Staffordshire

name and compl'ts to Mr W., with a desire to view his manufactory: in the mean time, I saunter'd about Mr W's grounds; which are green and pleasant, with some pretty plantations, views of the navigation etc. The house seems to be good, and is built of staring red brick; as are many in this vicinity belonging to the principal traders.[23]

After the completion of Bank House, all Pickford's efforts were concentrated on the pottery works. Wedgwood had received notice to quit Brick House, his existing works, and was clearly very worried. In November 1768 he wrote to his partner in a state of great agitation:

I have been confined to my room for several days planning with Mr Gardner the remainder of my works which must all be built besides a town for the men to live in by next summer. . . . where shall I get the money, materials and hands to finish so much building in so short a time?[24]

But all went well and the new Etruria Pottery finally opened on 13 June 1769.

Etruscan Works, Etruria, Staffordshire

To mark the occasion a special ceremony was held. Before a large assembly of friends and workmen Wedgwood threw the first pot while Bentley cranked the wheel.[25] After this the entire company retired to a place beneath the trees to enjoy the feast which Josiah had provided. It is not recorded if Pickford was present on this occasion.

In some ways the Etruscan Works were the most interesting part of the enterprise. We do not know which mill building was the first to be inspired by the works of Palladio, but Etruria was a very early example. In appearance it was thirteen bays long, three storeys high, with the central bay under a pediment, or rather a brick gable masquerading as a pediment, because the construction was no more complex than a field barn. The only architectural feature was the little cupola over the pediment. This housed the bell that summoned the workers to their toils.

From the first there was a lot of discussion about the design for the works. Bentley favoured a façade with a battlement,[26] which surely would have been the earliest example of a romantic solution for an industrial complex. As usual his ideas were rejected and the final design was without doubt Pickford's. In the years that followed many other industrial buildings were erected on the same principle. It was clear to all that the tenets of Palladio offered the mill owner the possibility of dignity without expense.

Apart from the work at Etruria, Pickford was also responsible for setting up Wedgwood's London showroom in Great Newport Street. On 30 April 1768 Wedgwood wrote to his London agent William Cox:

> I hope you are doing something towards my getting clear of the house at the bottom of St Martin's Lane. Every week I keep it on my hands it is near 20s. loss. I shall be content to part with it not being a loser.
>
> Mr Pickford, my architect, will be in town in about ten days and will call upon you and advise you about parting with the one and fitting up the other, in which article he says we are very likely to be imposed upon. He is a Londoner and knows all their tricks, and wishes to serve me in this or anything whilst he stays there.[27]

Wedgwood established his first London showroom in 1765, but following the execution of a tea service for Queen Charlotte, more suitable premises were rented in Charles Street, Grosvenor Square. By 1768 these too were deemed too small, as Wedgwood wanted 'to shew various Table and dessert services, completely set out on two ranges of Tables'. These requirements were ultimately met by the new showrooms in Great Newport Street, which opened in August 1768.[28]

Exactly what Pickford did towards achieving this is not recorded, but the final design incorporated a room where the finest pieces were kept in locked cases and shown only to privileged customers. This is the only recorded work that Pickford undertook in London, but there is reason to suppose that he maintained an interest there. Colvin records that he took as a pupil, James Pollard, a young student who was awarded premiums for architectural designs by the Society of Arts in 1764 and 1765. There is no record of Pollard living or working in Derby, but he was still in Pickford's employ in 1771, when Pickford asked Wedgwood for a bill to be made payable to Pollard, presumably in London, where he had some debts to settle.[29]

Among the many letters that Wedgwood wrote to his partner, two stand out because they give an insight into Pickford's character and business methods. The first is dated 20 June 1768:

> I shou'd like to have an estimate though Mr Pickford promised before he left to send me the particulars, he s'd he thought it not right to give such things to Noblemen or Gent'n as it hurt the neighbourhood, for the Gent'n wo'd afterwards expect his tenants to work for him as low as they did for the undertakers w'ch was not reasonable, as a Gent'n will not consider or allow for a mischance. . . . At the same time he assured me that he wo'd do my building upon much lower terms than he did for Gent'n. However there can be no harm in having a counter estimate and then I shall see more clearly how he befriends me.
>
> I am pleased with you feeling so much for the poor mortar maker, and will endeavour to set his mind at rest. Mr Pickford has much of the Bashaw in his treatment of workmen, and does not seem to consider their having any feelings at all. I have seen a great many instances of it and may sometime or other find out a mode of conveying a lecture to him upon the proper treatm't of our inferiors to prove that our humble friends have like passions to our selves . . .[30]

Bashaw, a corruption of Pasha, at that time summoned up the image of an oriental despot, cruel and indifferent to the suffering of others. If nothing else, it is clear from this description that Pickford was a hard master, but how much of Wedgwood's concern for the mortar man was real and how much was pure humbug is difficult to tell. Though in many ways Wedgwood was a humane employer he never allowed sentiment to stand in the way of profit. It is said in the army that the hardest officers are the ones who rise from the ranks. The mortar man may have been blameless, and Wedgwood's expressions of concern sincere, but Pickford understood what motivated his men and it is possible they respected him more because they knew he was one of them.

By the autumn of 1771 Pickford's reign at Etruria had come to an end. An acrimonious argument about replacing facing bricks to Etruria Hall was settled in Wedgwood's favour, as Pickford, as hard pressed for money as ever,

Engraving of the Etruscan Works, Etruria, Staffordshire

was anxious to settle the final account. Anyone in the building trade knows that this can be a wearisome business. Wedgwood knew Pickford's position and was determined to make the most of it. Their final meeting took place in April 1772:

> I should have written to my friend by Saturday's post, but for Mr Pickford coming here to settle our final accounts prevented me. The business took up one whole day and part of another. After deducting about £200 of his false and unreasonable charges . . . I have finally closed his account . . . in which I rejoice exceedingly. In one instance, for I will not trouble you with many I paid him for near 7000 bricks and laying . . . though he did not buy one from any other person. And for digging your cellars £6. This was left until the last article as I absolutely refused to allow it without your consent, upon which he declared he never would settle without having that extra digging allowed as he heard you himself and would take his oath upon it. He had several other persons who would swear you gave

orders for that particular work and if you did not allow it he would send to arrest you immediately. There's a genius for you, what chance do you think we should have where God swearing would carry it against us. Certainly none at all. I therefore submitted, but not without letting him know my opinion of his veracity upon that point. We did not finish until nearly nine at night, supper on the table, but the Knight and his squire Gardner would not wait a moment after the balance was paid, but marched away, dark as it was, to Newcastle, by which you may suppose we did not part in very good humour after our long sitting.[31]

In the building trade there is an old saying that the job is remembered long after the price has been forgotten. In Pickford's defence it can be argued that although Wedgwood said many disparaging things about his architect, his new house met with universal acclaim and Wedgwood seemed well contented with it. The smug tone of his letter to Bentley tells us that he had the best of the bargain, which he well knew.

CHAPTER NINE

Derby Friar Gate

In the summer of 1789 when Lord Torrington paid his first visit to Derby, he entered the town from the north passing as he said 'thro' Longley [Kirk Langley] and Markworth [Mackworth] below which in a vale is Mr Mundy's seat at Markeaton. . . . Derby looks well in approach, especially the steeple of All Saints church and the entering street is handsome.'[1] Although he does not say so this 'entering street' was Friar Gate, developed a few years earlier by the Trustees of Nun's Green and the setting of Joseph Pickford's own house.

Friar Gate, thanks mainly to Pickford's contribution, has one of the finest eighteenth-century street frontages in the county, and is a credit to the entrepreneurs of the time. The ground on which these houses were built was

Friar Gate

originally part of Nun's Green, a piece of common land on the north side of the town by the Ashbourne turnpike. By 1760 it had become an eyesore, a magnet for fly tippers and courting couples, and an embarrassment to the Corporation. To put the matter right an Act of Parliament was obtained in 1768 enabling the Corporation to set up an independent trust to sell off part of the Green to pay for the improvement of the remainder.

The part that was sold was the strip of land facing what is now Friar Gate, then the Ashbourne turnpike, where Pickford with a speculator's eye bought at least three plots. These were the sites for the houses now numbered 41, 44 and 45 Friar Gate, which, according to the deeds, he purchased in September 1768.[2] The conditions of sale called for the purchaser to erect within five years 'Dwelling Houses handsome in the Front towards the Publick Street . . . not less than three Storeys high and decently sasht.' A condition which Pickford more than adequately fulfilled.

There is no contemporary account of the building of Pickford's own house, number 41. All we know is that it was occupied by 1771.[3] Thomas Mozley, who visited the architect's son, the Revd Joseph Pickford in 1815,[4] tells us that:

> The father had built in the Friargate a house of some architectural pretensions, his *chef d'oeuvre*, people said. The son had divided it. He occupied the smaller portion, entered by the side door, much as it had come from the builder's hands . . . The larger part of the house and the front door he let . . . to Miss Knightley.

It was about this time that the houses in the street were numbered, Pickford's house being allocated numbers 40 and 41, to make allowance for the division. Today there is no number 40 Friar Gate.

Since the death of the Revd Joseph Pickford in 1844 the house has had many owners. The first person of note was Sir Thomas William Evans, MP, who was given his baronetcy by virtue of being mayor of Derby in the Golden Jubilee year of 1887.[5] Then it passed to W.G. Curgenven, a noted surgeon and Derbyshire cricketer, and after him to other surgeons, until appropriately it was acquired by a firm of architects in 1953. It is now the property of the City of Derby and was opened to the public in 1988 as the Pickford House Museum.

The front façade facing the street is the culmination of a series of designs, including the Hodgson House and the Mansion in Ashbourne, Ogston Hall near Chesterfield, and Sandon Hall, Staffordshire, which was completed a year or so later. The basic elements are the same with a combination of Diocletian and Venetian windows and a tripartite door, but the house in Friar Gate has far more finesse. Like the Mansion it has an open pediment filled with brick voussoirs, but there the comparison ends. The Mansion is only an

No. 41 Friar Gate, Derby

Detail of the door surround, No. 41
Friar Gate, Derby

apprentice piece, but No. 41 Friar Gate is the culmination of years of study. In
a sense it is his *chef d'oeuvre* because it is by far the finest of his brick façades,
and though he was to attempt similar things in the future he never again
approached the quality he achieved here.

The façade needs no explanation, but the details repay careful study. The
frieze to the tripartite door surround is of great interest. As befits an architect,
the ornamental panels between the swags display groups of architectural
drawing instruments. At first it was thought these might relate to the practice
of Freemasonry, but it has now emerged that although the elements, like
squares and compasses, are significant, the order in which they are arranged is
not.[6]

Also of interest are the tall vases with wavy, striated surfaces, which stand at
each end of the frieze. There are a number of precedents for this design. John
Vardy in his volume, *Some Designs of Mr Inigo Jones and Mr William Kent*,
published in 1744, a source book much used by Pickford, shows a vase, one of
a pair, with similar surface treatment, which Vardy describes as 'Two vases
with pedestals for Mr Pope.'

This same vase appears again on the memorial plaque to Richard Wright in
St Michael's church in Derby. Wright, who died in December 1770, was first

cousin to the father of Joseph Wright, and though he had a country seat at Loaden Hall, Staffordshire,[7] he practised in Derby and probably found many of his patients among the friends of his family. It seems likely that this monument was designed by Pickford at the same time as the house in Friar Gate.

After the street façade the interior is in some ways an anticlimax. Clearly Pickford lavished his all on the outside, leaving next to nothing to complete the reception rooms. Still the hall and the drawing room, though very restrained, rank among the finest interiors in the town.

As at St Helen's and the Hodgson House, in Friar Gate the architect followed the same plan, setting the staircase in a separate compartment off the rear of the hall. The hall itself is simple, but effective, decorated with swags and paterae depicting the muses, and musical instruments. There are four internal doors leading from the hall, two to the reception rooms facing the street, which are unadorned, and two to the rooms at the rear.

On the left is the dining room with three windows on the long elevation overlooking the garden. The walls are plain save for a plaster modillion cornice, but the chimney-piece on the end wall is of the very best quality. It, too, is simply conceived with no sculptural ornament except for the vases each

The entrance hall ceiling, No. 41 Friar Gate, Derby

105

Drawing room chimney-piece, No. 41 Friar
Gate, Derby

side of the frieze. The chimney-piece itself is of white Carrara marble with inset
panels of yellow Siena and glyphs inlaid with Derbyshire Blue John. It was in
this room that Mrs Pickford introduced Bagshaw Stevens to the Derby Rout.

Next to the drawing room is the compartment containing the staircase,
which is of the cantilevered type in Hopton Wood stone with a wrought-iron
balustrade. This has plain square bars to the steps and wave bars on the
landing. The wave bar was a distinguishing feature of the work of the
celebrated smith, Robert Bakewell of Derby, who died in 1752. In 1770 his old
foreman Benjamin Yates was still in business at his shop in the Wardwick,[8] a
stone's throw away, so there can be little doubt it was Yates, or one of his sons,
who was responsible for the ironwork. At the bottom of the stairs it is still
possible to see where the dog-gate was fitted, suggesting that the collie in
Wright's portrait of the Pickford children was a real family pet.

It is of interest that Pickford, with such a fine craftsman as Benjamin Yates
at his disposal, should have been content with such run-of-the-mill ironwork. It
is true that elaborate ironwork was at that time out of fashion, but Pickford's
restraint more likely reflects the fact that the staircase, separated from the
reception rooms, was not generally used by visitors. Certainly he never
completed the rooms on the upper floors, which to this day are plain and
bereft of ornament.

Detail of the chimney-piece, No. 41 Friar Gate, Derby

The right-hand flight of stairs leads down to the cellar and out into the garden through a loggia with three semi-circular arches corresponding to the drawing-room windows above. The rear elevation, though dignified in proportion, is completely plain save for the arcade which today fronts a dingy area and the cellar wall. When the house was built this was probably a pleasant sitting space, but today the architect's intentions are difficult to define.

Before Agard Street at the rear was laid out in 1793,[9] there was no access to the garden and the workshop except through the archway of No. 45, which Pickford reserved for himself when he sold the plot.[10] Perhaps he never intended the garden to be anything other than a builder's yard. Certainly he was content to have his workshop and his building materials in his eye where he could see them. After his death the notice of the sale of his stock showed this to be the usual builder's bric-a-brac, including scaffold poles and the like, so there would have been very little room left for a formal garden.

Next door but one to Pickford's house is No. 44 Friar Gate, which was built by Pickford for John Ward, a silk throwster, and a tradesman of the town. Pickford purchased the plot in September 1768 and sold it the following year to Ward,[11] doubtless with a clause that he should be the architect and builder of the new house. This property, like No. 41, was occupied in 1771.[12]

No. 44 Friar Gate, Derby

The design of the street façade is of particular interest because it is a close copy of the Beresford House built a year or two earlier in the Compton at Ashbourne. Both houses are three bays wide and three storeys high with the same combination of Venetian windows and recessed blank arches at first-floor level, but with one important difference; the house in Friar Gate is in brick, the one in the Compton in stone. This seems to have a profound effect upon the character of the buildings; the stone façade being sombre and masculine, and the brick one delicate and feminine. Apart from that there is only one significant difference. At Ashbourne the modillion cornice is placed between the first and second storeys, at Friar Gate it is above the second storey.

The plan of the house is unremarkable, though in this case the cantilevered stone staircase, with a wrought-iron balustrade similar to No. 41, is situated in the main hallway. The reception rooms have fine plaster cornices and there is some good quality joinery, though by and large the interior, like that of No. 41, was finished on a shoe-string budget.

The history of No. 44 Friar Gate after the death of John Ward in 1785 is of little interest. The house remained in the family for more than a hundred years until it, too, was purchased by a surgeon in 1891. After that it ceased to be a private dwelling and was used exclusively for commercial purposes. At one time in the 1920s it was a 'Swedish Gymnasium' and later a school of dancing. Since then it has passed to more orthodox professions and is now the office of a publisher.[13]

The plot of No. 45 Friar Gate was also purchased by Pickford in September 1768 and sold on in January 1771 to Daniel Lowe, a hosier, and the partner of John Ward who built the house next door. Contrary to the conditions of sale, they then erected a mill on the site, an undertaking in which Pickford had a hand as he retained for himself the right of access over the land. What Pickford's interest in the business was we cannot say, but we do know that after his death his wife Mary was involved in the manufacture of worsted. She and a partner named Thomas Barber had a mill on Nun's Green until 1786 when the partnership was dissolved and Mrs Pickford carried on the business in her own name.[14]

The flagrant abuse of the sale conditions by Pickford and Lowe could not have helped neighbourly relations. Clearly there was much ill feeling and possibly legal action, as in June 1778 Lowe sold the mill to his partner, John Ward[15] who later converted it into a dwelling house. However, not much thought was put into the conversion, as the street façade is the plainest in the row.

This was in part remedied by the distinguished Derby architect, Henry Isaac Stevens, who purchased the property in 1872.[16] It was either Stevens or his partner, Frederick Robinson, who added the redbrick, neo-Romanesque porch, which still adorns the front today. After Robinson the property inevitably passed to another surgeon, which helped to give Friar Gate the reputation of being the Harley Street of Derby.

Since Pickford's time Friar Gate has had fluctuating fortunes. The money obtained from the sale for the improvement of Nun's Green convinced the Corporation that they had discovered an easy way of raising revenue without milking the ratepayers. In 1792 a second Act was obtained to sell off the remainder of the Green to pay for paving and lighting the streets of Derby. This was carried through in the face of bitter opposition, for the critics feared that within a generation the ground flanking Markeaton Brook would be filled with unsightly mills and warehouses. How right this prophesy proved to be. Much to the consternation of the gentry, Willow Row and Brook Street soon became notorious for drunken Irishmen fighting it out with the Peelers, a reputation the area has carried almost to the present day. Yet, perhaps this case is overstated as Friar Gate itself has always been considered a genteel street. At least one visitor to the town thought so, Sir Richard Phillips writing in the early nineteenth century noted:

> One broad street, called Friar Gate, above half a mile long, is filled with tasteful mansions, and similar structures, in the architectural style of the early years of George the Third. Some of them are occupied . . . by persons of fortune who find in Derby, the agreeableness of town and country.[17]

It seems to us remarkable that such genteel people were prepared to live cheek by jowl with the roughnecks of the town. But this was prior to the age of the motor car, when urban areas were much smaller than they are today, and people, of necessity, lived much closer together.

CHAPTER TEN

Sandon Hall and Other Country Villas, 1768–72

The constant cajoling of potential clients with drawings and promises though unethical by modern professional standards is effective if pursued with vigour as any salesman will testify. By 1768 Pickford was sufficiently established to rely on his reputation and the good opinion of others to make his contacts, but he still had to convince his potential clients that he was more than a common builder. This he achieved by the quality of his designs. Though he never attempted to make his living purely by architecture, which at this date in the provinces would have been hard to achieve, none the less, his gentlemen clients and contemporaries seemed to accept him as a man of taste and a good judge of architecture. More than likely this was because he was able to portray himself as a metropolitan, closely associated with the great buildings of the day.

One commission which came to Pickford more or less out of the blue, and eventually led to further work, was for Sandon Hall, five miles north of Stafford, and half a day's ride from Etruria where he was working at the time. His client was Lord Archibald Hamilton (1740–1819), the brother of the Duke of Hamilton and the brother-in-law of John Leveson-Gower, Earl Gower of Trentham. The house Pickford designed for him at Sandon was destroyed by fire in 1848, but Pickford's drawings survive,[1] and the building was included by James Gandon in volume V of *Vitruvius Britannicus*.

Apparently Pickford was not the only architect angling for the job. Sir William Chambers also submitted a design,[2] as he wrote to Lord Archibald in July 1772 requesting payment of his bill for £43, which presumably was for drawings commissioned a year or so before. Pickford's design was probably preferred because he worked locally and was prepared to build at lower rates than his rivals, but it illustrates the point that he was considered by potential clients as the equal of London professionals.

There was nothing fancy about Sandon Hall, it was a straightforward five-bay villa with pavilion wings connected to the main house with single storey

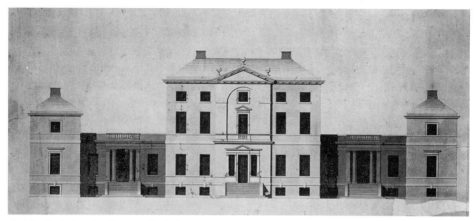

Pickford's design for Sandon Hall, Staffordshire

links. As it was only intended for hunting parties it was constructed without great expense in redbrick with stone dressings, but like all of Pickford's designs it was well proportioned and, on paper at least, looked very stylish.

In appearance the main front was almost identical to Pickford's own house in Derby, so we know more or less what it looked like. A comparison is interesting because we can see how the architect transformed a town house into a country villa, with the simple addition of wings and pavilions. It must be admitted that the design would have been improved if the pavilions had been brought forward or set back, and connected with curved link corridors. Pickford would certainly have known this, but if cash limits are imposed on the architect they will certainly affect the quality of the design.

If the façade was like the house in Friar Gate, the interior was far more interesting. The plan of the ground floor, which we know from *Vitruvius Britannicus*, was a vast improvement on any of his earlier designs. A section drawn through the house gives us a glimpse of the interior. From the entrance hall a visitor passed through an Ionic screen into the top lit staircase compartment in the centre of the house, and on through a pedimented doorway into the drawing room. The staircase itself was semi-circular on plan and at right angles to the main axis running from the front to the rear of the house. For the first time in a newly built house Pickford breaks away from the conventional collection of rectangular compartments. Apart from a semi-circular staircase he also provided Lord Archibald with an octagonal dressing room, not unlike Dr Taylor's garden room at Ashbourne.

No documentation for the building, apart from the drawings, has survived, but several letters written by Pickford and his assistant, Thomas Gardner, to Josiah Wedgwood are post-dated from Sandon and show that the house was under construction between April 1770 and December 1771.³ In April 1770 Wedgwood wrote to his partner Bentley about the £200 they owed Pickford which he had refused to pay to Pickford's assistant, Thomas Gardner, at Etruria. He says, 'I suppose Mr Pickford will call for it immediately to send to Mr Gardner as he wants to pay the workmen at Sandon.' Nothing could better illustrate Pickford's recurring problem of being forced to beg money from one client to finance building work for another.

Shortly after Sandon was built Lord Archibald sold it to Nathaniel Ryder, the father of Dudley Ryder, the first Earl of Harrowby, who mentioned the house in his autobiography.⁴ Dudley went up to Cambridge in 1779, but spent his vacations at Sandon where he helped his father with the improvements he was making to the house. This work is dated between 1777 and 1784, and Samuel Wyatt was the architect. Ryder tells us that 'There were many improvements going on to the house and grounds . . . when the house was bought my father found the place nearly as it is now to the exterior, but the only habitable part was the centre and the octagon room below.' By this he meant that the two wings were still service areas as Pickford intended. These were now turned into reception rooms which involved the removal of the porches in the link blocks and building new walls in front to form corridors.

Engraving of Sandon Hall, Staffordshire

Nathaniel Ryder discussed these improvements with King George III[5] who considered himself to be a good judge of architecture. He 'expressed the fear that by destroying or diminishing the break, the front would be made too flat'. In this the king was certainly right, and Wyatt should have known better than to strip off what little architectural ornament the house possessed. Lord Harrowby thought the house was not worth including in *Vitruvius Britannicus*, but he does write of it with great affection, suggesting it was at least for him a congenial place to live.

At least one discerning traveller was also suitably impressed. Lord Torrington, a harsh critic of modern architecture, riding from Stone to Ingestre in 1792, passed through Sandon and noted the appearance of the house and gardens, which he recorded with some pleasure:

> I now come to Sandon village; beyond which is Sandon Hall, the seat of Ld Harrowby: This is a new made place, with young healthy plantations: the house to which I rode, seems good, and is placed, a la mode, on the hill-top.[6]

Like Etruria the park at Sandon was the work of William Emes. According to a recent study it was laid out in 1771 for Lord Harrowby.[7] If this was the case he must have bought the house before the building works were complete.

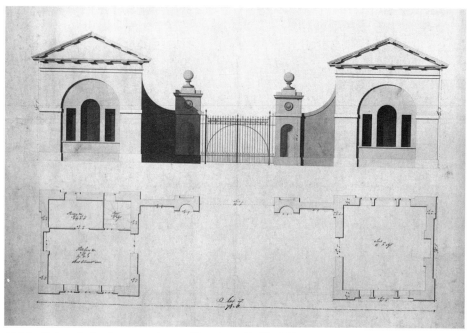

Pickford's first design for a gate house, Trentham, Staffordshire

The building of Sandon Hall led to a small commission from another prestigious client, Granville Leveson-Gower (1721–1803) who succeeded to the title and estate at Trentham in 1754. The 2nd Earl was a great patron of architecture. He built Gower House in Whitehall, and at Trentham, between 1775 and 1778, he employed Capability Brown and Henry Holland to carry out extensions to the house and improvements to the park. A year or so before he had engaged Pickford to design two gate lodges, the drawings of which are now at the Staffordshire Record Office.[8]

In the eighteenth century the entrance to Trentham Park was from the south, through the village of Tittensor. It was on this road that Pickford built his lodges. He submitted two designs: the first was a straight copy of William Kents's north lodges at Holkham in Norfolk;[9] the second design is more original, though its most distinctive feature, the semi-circular gate arches, were taken from Kent's design for the gate between the Boycott Pavilions at Stowe in Buckinghamshire.[10] Pickford was not particular as even the horseman passing through the gate belonged to Kent, or rather to Vardy, who first published the design. The building as it was erected contained elements from both drawings.

Lord Torrington passing that way after his sighting of Sandon Hall in 1792 noted the gate houses on the road to Tittensor, but did not regard them as being worthy of comment. It was the park that caught his eye, and the work of

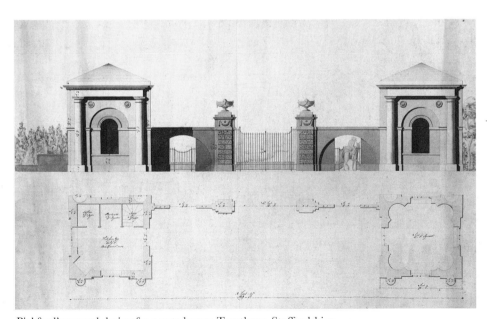

Pickford's second design for a gate house, Trentham, Staffordshire

his old friend 'Launcelot Brown, who is to be traced at every turn: he, certainly, was a grand planner, a leveller of ground, and a judicious former of water'. In this case it would seem that Pickford and Emes were deposed in favour of Brown and Holland.[11]

An almost identical set of gates and lodges to those at Trentham stand at the entrance to Brocket Hall in Hertfordshire, rebuilt by James Paine, for Sir Matthew Lamb, and his son Peniston Lamb, later Viscount Melbourne in 1760–75. According to Colvin, Paine was also responsible for the entrance screen and gates, and we see no reason to question his authority except for an unusual payment to Pickford in the Melbourne Hall accounts for 1773: 'Paid Mr Pickford for making drawings for Brocket Hall £21.'[12]

Viscount Melbourne took the name of his title from the small Derbyshire town where his family had owned property for nearly two hundred years. And though they lived mainly in London and at Brocket, they took a lively interest in their Derbyshire estates and were patrons of both Pickford and Joseph Wright. As early as 1770 Pickford was making designs for unspecified rooms at Melbourne,[13] though the only work he seems to have done there was to reroof the Hall in 1773,[14] the same year he was paid for the drawings at Brocket. To employ two architects on one contract is unethical to say the least, but 1773 is the right year for the gates and screen, and the finished work at Brocket bears an uncanny likeness to Pickford's gates at Trentham.

Engraving of Wanlip Hall, Leicestershire

Another country villa similar in size and appearance to Sandon was Wanlip Hall, pleasantly situated on the River Soar about five miles north of Leicester. According to John Nichols, writing in 1804,[15] Henry Palmer Esq. demolished the old Hall in 1768, before 'erecting the present spacious and substantial house on the site of the old one'. At this date, as far as we know, Pickford had not been involved with any building in Leicestershire, but the year before, in 1767, he had submitted designs for the new Leicester Infirmary.[16] The contract for the infirmary was awarded to William Henderson of Loughborough working under the direction of Benjamin Wyatt. Though Pickford was not successful on this occasion his entry may have brought his skills to the attention of the gentlemen of the county.

Nichols goes on to recount that 'In 1775 Wanlip became the property of Charles Grave(s) Hudson (FRS) [the husband of Palmer's daughter], who completed the building at Wanlip with many additions and improvements to the original plan. The building was originally of brick, but has since been stuccoed and is seen at great advantage from the Melton Road.' The front that Nichols refers to is yet another replica of the house in Friar Gate, with similar wings and pavilions to Sandon. The only difference being that the ornamental door surrounds in the connecting wings at Sandon were changed to linked arches at Wanlip.

Another illustration by Throsby of 1789,[17] shows the garden front more or less as it was designed with a central canted bay not unlike Tissington Hall in Derbyshire. This seems to have been a feature which Pickford liked as it appears on a number of his designs. It is not an inspired innovation, but at least it breaks up a flat elevation and enables the architect to improve his plan at no great expense.

CHAPTER ELEVEN

St Mary's Church, Birmingham

St Mary's Whittall Street, Birmingham, Pickford's only known attempt at ecclesiastical architecture, was demolished in 1925 to make way for an extension to the General Hospital. During its lifetime, the building suffered greatly at the hands of insensitive restorers who had little or no sympathy for classical architecture. Most of the improvements were cosmetic, but in 1866 the master-stroke was delivered when the steeple was taken down and replaced with a Gothic spire. It was all a far cry from the day in August 1774, at the Bishop's consecration, when the *Birmingham Gazette*, with pardonable exaggeration, called the building 'the wonder of the age'.[1]

In keeping with St Mary's sad decline, it does not come as a surprise to be told that the building committee's minute book was rescued by an architectural enthusiast from a wartime salvage dump. It has since been lost again, but not before another enthusiast, the late Revd Basil Clarke, took some notes from it. What little information we have about St Mary's building history, we owe to him.[2]

The history of Birmingham and its growth from a modest village to the second city of the kingdom in the space of two hundred years is outside the scope of this book, but a few facts are necessary to understand how St Mary's fitted in with the overall development. Before 1600 Birmingham was a rural community of no importance centred on the parish church of St Martin. The Bull Ring, now a shopping precinct, was then the village green. Throughout the seventeenth century the village expanded in a northerly direction, first to take in the new parish of St Philip's, consecrated in 1715, and then along Steel House Lane on to the Weaman Estate by the new General Hospital, which was begun in 1766, but not opened until 1779.[3]

With the growth of population the need for a new church became a matter of some concern. St Mary's was consecrated in 1774, as a Chapel of Ease to St Philip's and did not become an independent parish until the nineteenth century. Both St Mary's and St Paul's,[4] a second chapel built 1777–9, were the result of public agitation and strenuous efforts on the part of the building committee to raise the necessary funds.

The first public meeting to consider the new chapel was held at the Old Cross Chambers in the Bull Ring on 15 October 1771. As an Act of Parliament was required, it was resolved to apply for two new churches in Birmingham, though at this stage they had neither land nor money for either. To overcome this difficulty, a formidable committee, ninety strong, was formed 'to transact and forward the necessary business' and 'to open a public subscription for the purpose of building the said chapels'.[5]

By 1 December only £251 had been received, but then things improved, as at the next meeting we are told that members of the committee had waited on Miss Weaman who had promised to subscribe £1,200 and give 2½ acres of land for the chapel and burial ground. The Bill was presented to Parliament in February 1772 and the Act was passed in June. Finally it was resolved to commence building work as soon as £3,000 had been promised.

It is not clear who advised the committee on building matters, but they had a clear idea of what they wanted before the architect was appointed. On 4 November 1772 it was resolved that the chapel should take the form of 'an octagon galleried around and finished with a tower in proportion to the building'. The whole was to be built with brick except the 'stone cills, battlement walls and frontispieces'. At this point a small crumb was thrown to the architect when it was decided that the pillars should be left to his judgement, but not the number of seats, which was fixed at 1,000. These were 'each to be 22 inches wide, and wainscotted with oak'. The total cost was estimated at between £3,000 and £4,000.[6]

The idea of the octagonal plan was probably suggested to the committee by the famous octagonal Nonconformist chapel in Norwich, built by the architect Thomas Ivory (1709–79), between the years 1754 and 1756. For a provincial architect this had an ambitious interior with giant Corinthian columns supporting the dome. The advantage of such a shape is that it gives the maximum clear space for both seeing and hearing a point of some importance in a service where the focus of attention is the preacher delivering a sermon.

Five days later on 9 November an advertisement was placed in the *Birmingham Gazette*:

> . . . We do hereby request any architect or builder capable of such an undertaking to send or deliver Plans Elevations & Estimates, sealed up to Mr John Cottrell . . . on or before the 22nd of January next, for building one of the said chapels, as no plans etc. will be received after that day. The said chapel to be built in an octagon or any other form as the said architect shall think proper, and to contain 1000 sittings . . . For any further particulars apply to the said John Cottrell.

The notes made from the minutes by Mr Clarke do not indicate what

Engraving of St Mary's church, Birmingham

response this advertisement produced, only that the trustees considered 'a plan exhibited by Mr Joseph Pickford of Derby', and that his estimate of £3,666 18s. 6d. was accepted. At the same meeting a Mr Thomas Saul was appointed to inspect the workmanship and materials and an allowance of ten guineas was made by the trustees for his trouble.

Unfortunately Mr Clarke gives no date for this meeting or any further details, but the implication seems to be that Pickford presented his drawings in person, which suggests he knew in advance that his tender would be accepted. As it is highly unlikely that he was the only one to submit drawings he must have had foreknowledge of the committee's deliberations. With a group that size it is difficult to keep matters secret, but there must have been a person or faction on it that favoured Pickford's design.

Mr Clarke says of the committee, 'that it is a formidable list, but I have given it in full to illustrate a considerable body of the more important citizens of that time, because many of them are Birmingham names that have endured to this day.'

From this mass of Birmingham worthies a few names stand out. Edmund

Hector (1708–94) was by profession a surgeon, but is best remembered today as being the lifelong friend of Dr Johnson. Indeed, Hector was the nephew of the man-midwife who delivered Johnson. He was also well known to Matthew Boulton and other members of the Lunar Society. In 1776, when Johnson and Boswell stayed in Birmingham, it was Hector who conducted Boswell on a visit to Boulton's Soho manufactory.[7]

Edmund Hector's sister Anne married a clergyman named Careless; by this date she was a widow, but doubtless Thomas Careless, another member of the building committee, was related to her, and was possibly her son. Of Anne Hector, Johnson told Boswell that if he had married her 'it might have been as happy' for him.[8] But instead he married Tetty Porter, the widow of a Birmingham mercer. The committee member Joseph Porter was probably related to her first husband.

Thomas Bingham was born in Derby,[9] and had a brother and cousins who still lived there, but the pair most likely to have formed the Pickford faction were John Ash and Thomas Gisborne. Ash we know had been acquainted with the architect for some years. When Pickford wrote to Matthew Boulton in 1760, he added as a postscript to his letter, 'Please give my Duty to Dr Ash etc.'[10]

Dr John Ash (1723–98) was an eminent physician and one of the founders of the General Hospital. Though not of the Lunar Society, he was well known to the other members and attended their meetings as a guest. His particular friend was William Small (1734–75), with whom he shared his house and practice.

Small was educated at Aberdeen University and from 1764 to 1768 was Professor of Natural Philosophy at the College of William and Mary in Virginia.[11] In 1764 he returned to England and in the following year was introduced, by a letter from Franklin, to Boulton, whose family physician he then became. He was interested in steam engines, chemistry, clocks and optics, and found great pleasure in the company of his fellow Lunatics, especially James Watt and John Whitehurst.

Dr Thomas Gisborne, like John Ash, was another leading physician associated with the General Hospital. Though there is no evidence of any direct contact with Pickford, he was born in Derby,[12] the son of the rector of Staveley, and first cousin of John Gisborne, the builder of St Helen's House. Later in life he became physician to the king, and the president of the Royal College of Physicians.

In the minutes there is no record of building progress, but work must have started in the spring of 1773, as six months later, on 7 September, the trustees voted that 'five guineas be given to the workmen as a treat for rearing the said chapel'. By this date the roof spanning the sixty-foot octagon must have been in place. As the building is now gone it is not possible to comment on Pickford's method of construction, but covering such an area without supports must have taxed his ingenuity as well as his nerve.

The best illustration of St Mary's chapel was engraved from a drawing of 1842 by Henry Burn. Assuming his proportions are correct, the tower, with the entrances through porches on each side, was very awkward and ill-proportioned. Unless it was part of the brief, it is difficult to see why Pickford chose this form of access in preference to the more conventional doorway in the base of the tower. One explanation could be that the separate entrances served different parts of the building; one door to the main body of the chapel and the other to the gallery. The octagon, in plain redbrick, with widely-spaced windows, was sombre and overbearing, forcing one to agree with the critic who thought the building was not overcharged with light.[13]

St Mary's chapel was consecrated by the Bishop of Lichfield on St Bartholomew's Day, 24 August 1774. On 2 September the *Derby Mercury* quoted with some pride the description of the opening in the *Birmingham Gazette*:

On Wednesday St Mary's Chapel in Birmingham was opened and Divine Service read for the first time . . . The said chapel has been about seventeen months in building and contains in the seats about one thousand and seventy places. The plan on which it is built is admirably well adapted for hearing, and the whole building is executed in a masterly manner. Witness that surprising roof which is the wonder of the age and covers an octagon building of upwards of eighty feet in diameter, without one pillar to support it, and every other part so well performed as to redound greatly to the honour of that celebrated and ingenious architect Mr Joseph Pickford of Derby.[14]

Not everyone was as kind as the *Birmingham Gazette*. William Hutton, the antiquarian, was very offhand. He thought the building ' . . . shows too little steeple and too much roof. If a light balustrade was raised over the parapet with an urn in the centre of the roof, the eye of the observer would be relieved'.[15] This we consider to be a just criticism, but instead of leaving the matter there he could not resist adding a sarcastic comment: 'The clock was seldom seen to go right, but the wonder ceases if there are no works within.' Hutton does not mention the architect by name, which is unusual as he himself was a Derbian. It is not known if there was any personal animosity between them, but in his *History of Derby*, Hutton also fails to mention Pickford by name, though he does have a number of unkind things to say about his buildings. That Hutton knew Pickford, or knew of him, cannot be doubted, as George Moneypenny, a close associate of the Derby architect, engraved the plates for Hutton's history of his native town.

J.M. Brindley, an unbiased reporter, writing a hundred years after St Mary's was built, at a time when classical churches were not in fashion, spoke surprisingly well of it:

> The interior has a broad central aisle leading to a richly decorated chancel. The somewhat formal interior is relieved by tasteful decorations which are strictly in keeping with the design of the building. The panels of the old high backed pews are beaded with gold. The pulpit and gallery are also beaded with gold and a handsome organ occupies the west gallery.[16]

Shortly after the chapel was opened, part of the gallery collapsed, which must have made the parishioners a little apprehensive about the rest of the structure. Roger Eykyn of Wolverhampton was called in to advise upon it,[17] which probably explains why Eykyn and not Pickford was appointed architect for the next chapel to be built under the Act, St Paul's, in 1776.

In the light of Pickford's known connection with Dr Ash, it is possible he had an involvement with the building of the Birmingham General Hospital, on the ground next to the chapel. Ash was the driving force behind the project, and was responsible for calling the public meeting in 1765, which set the matter afoot. At first all went well, £2,000 was raised, and an 8-acre site purchased. Work began in 1766, but rather like the Derby Assembly Rooms, it was stopped shortly afterwards when the funds ran out. From 1769 until 1776 the building stood half finished, when, with the help of a musical festival, fresh money was raised and it was finally completed in 1779.[18]

The opening after thirteen years of concerted effort was a curiously low-key affair. The *Birmingham Gazette* reported on 4 October 1779: 'The General Hospital near this town opened on Wednesday last and Saturday being the day appointed for admission of patients several persons recommended were received within.' There was no display of civic pride, no grand opening, only a reminder to the patients to bring their clean linen. What Dr Ash thought on the matter is not recorded.

The building itself was aggressively plain, the sort of barrack block that gave charity a bad name. It was nine bays wide, three storeys high, and stood on a basement within an area which was railed around. The three central bays projected forward under a pediment, with a central doorway opening on to a bridge which spanned the area. According to the illustrator, apart from the surround to the door the building displayed no ornamental features whatsoever. Any builder might have designed it, and if Pickford was responsible it is certainly not something he would have remembered with pride. Two wings, as plain as the original, were added in 1790.

If Whittall Street had remained a quiet suburb, St Mary's would probably have survived intact, but nineteenth-century industrial development put paid to that. As the century advanced conditions around the church grew worse. The minute book lists numerous complaints about acts of vandalism committed by thoughtless schoolboys, until in 1836 the churchyard was closed as a public thoroughfare. Things had improved by 1882, when the burial ground was laid out as a public garden which Basil Clarke visited after the Second World War. Then, as he put it, 'part of the burial ground was still an open space, albeit a very shabby one, made worse by the removal of the iron railings'. Apart from that all he could find 'were a few gravestones and monuments tumbled about'.

Today it is still possible to see where St Mary's church once stood, but only just. St Mary's Row and Whittall Street, which formed the north-west angle of the churchyard, still survive, though a little further on both of these thoroughfares are bisected by a motorway which effectively prevents further exploration in that direction. On the site of the church there is a multi-storey car park to serve the needs of the hospital, and behind that some temporary buildings. The only part of the churchyard now standing is a short length of boundary wall by St Mary's Row, but doubtless that will be removed as soon as the finances of the General Hospital allow.

CHAPTER TWELVE

Wirksworth Moot Hall
and Trinity Hospital, Leicester

The two buildings commissioned by the Duchy of Lancaster from Pickford, Wirksworth Moot Hall[1] and Trinity Hospital, Leicester,[2] have long since been demolished. All that remains today is a bundle of letters and drawings among the Duchy papers at the Public Record Office. Yet in one sense we know more about these two buildings than almost anything else he designed. The drawings show his true intentions, and the correspondence, the day-to-day problems that were the lot of any architect before the advent of modern transport and systems of communication.

At the Trinity Hospital he was called on to rebuild a medieval almshouse, a project of no great architectural interest. But the Moot Hall was a building of merit, and its passing was a great loss to Wirksworth. As an essay in civic design it was on a modest scale, though if the drawings are anything to go by what Pickford achieved at Wirksworth for £742 was quite remarkable.

The Enclosure Award Map of 1806 shows that it stood in front of the Red Lion Inn on the north side of the Market Place. The *Universal British Directory* of 1792 tells us that it was erected in 1773, and in 1811 a local historian described the building as 'a respectable structure in brick',[3] though we now know it was dignified with stone dressings.

The building was a success, though the siting of it was clearly a mistake. Soon after it was finished the townspeople were complaining of the congestion caused by the lead miners bringing their carts to the court. Pressure was mounted for its removal, and in 1814[4] the building was demolished and a new hall erected in Chapel Lane. Today all that remains of Pickford's building are two bas-relief plaques that were reset in the façade of the new hall.

The Moot, or Barmoot Court, at Wirksworth has a long history. In 1288 Edward I ordered an inquisition to be held at Ashbourne to define the claims of the Derbyshire lead miners. The outcome was that the lead mining areas of the county were divided into Liberties, each served by a Barmoot Court,

Pickford's design for the Wirksworth Moot Hall (principal elevation)

presided over by the Barmaster, usually a solicitor, who had the power to regulate the industry in the 'King's Field', that is the Crown concession in the Peak District.

The original Wirksworth Moot Hall was a medieval timber-framed structure. The court room was at first-floor level and stood on an open arcade, which on market days served as a cover to the butchers' stalls. Nothing more is known of this building except that in 1608 it was described as being in a state of great decay, so it is not surprising that by 1770 the Duchy thought it was time to take it down.

The first notice the public received that Moot Hall was to be replaced was an advertisement in the *Derby Mercury* on 13 May 1771. This is worth quoting in full:

Notice is hereby given that the old Moot Hall in the town of Wirksworth is to be wholly taken down and a new Moot Hall erected in its stead as soon as a plan and estimate are fixed upon for that purpose. Such persons who are willing to undertake this work are desired to deliver a tender to Mr John Goodwin of Ashbourne on or before the 7th day of June next, with an estimate for completing the same with stone and tile or slate as they will abide by and the person whose plan and estimate meet with approbation may depend on being preferred and treated with immediately.

John Goodwin was at that time Barmaster of the Wirksworth Liberty.

It is not known how many tenders were submitted, but on 8 July 1772 the contract was awarded to James Eglington for the sum of £749 11s. 4d.[5] This James Eglington was probably a son of a Northamptonshire stone mason, Benjamin Eglington of Badby. Benjamin Eglington junior, buried in St Werburgh's church, Derby, in August 1768, and Samuel Eglington, buried at Ashbourne in December 1788,[6] if not his brothers, were certainly his kinsmen. The best-known member of their family, Joseph Eglington (1746–1810) of Coventry, designed the County Hall in that city, and was a gentleman of means. His kinsman was not so successful either as an architect or as a businessman. James Eglington's design for Moot Hall is a weak attempt in the conventional Palladian style, an updated version of the existing building.

Nothing further happened until June 1773, when it is recorded that James Eglington was dead, and that the contract had been relet to 'Joseph Pickford of Derby, architect' for the sum of £742,[7] slightly less than the original estimate. The Duchy was clearly pleased with its new bargain, as the minutes note: 'compared with the former plan appearing before this court it is in many ways preferable and better calculated for the intended uses'.

How Pickford became involved is not explained in the Duchy Revenue Proceedings. It is clear his design was new to the committee, so he was

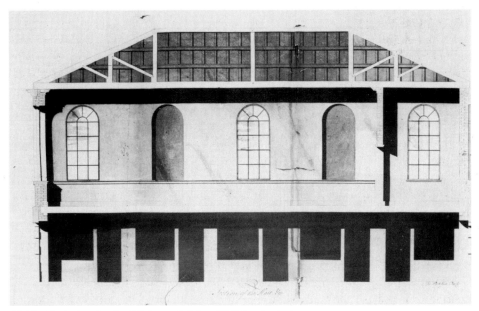

Pickford's design for the Wirksworth Moot Hall (section)

Moot Hall (end elevation)

probably invited, after Eglington's death, to submit a scheme he was prepared to build for the sum already approved.

Pickford's design for Moot Hall owed much to the Lutheran Chapel in the Savoy, which his kinsman, James Pickford, built in 1766 to the designs of the architect, Sir William Chambers.[8] Like Chambers, Pickford had a preference for antique Roman forms which gave his buildings great dignity, ideally suited for civic architecture.

The only oddity in the design is the curious pediment, triangular in shape with the apex taken off parallel to the base of the triangle. Sir William Chambers in his book on *Civil Architecture* gives it as one of the types of pediment to be avoided, but he does not tell us if it had a precedent in antiquity. Pickford's development of the basic idea results in a balustrade with triangular blocks on each side looking rather like bookends.

The other feature of interest on the façade are the two carved panels which were reset on the new building. The name of the sculptor is not known, but it was almost certainly George Moneypenny, the architect's associate in Derby. The plaques are richly carved to Pickford's design and show the cap of Liberty, the scales of Justice, the standard measure for the lead bar and the Roman fasces, a symbol of authority not then burdened with the unsavoury reputation it carries today.

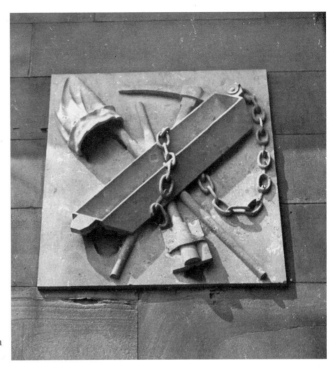

Plaque from the Wirksworth
Moot Hall

The correspondence in the Duchy archive all dates from after the completion of Moot Hall, but it does include a defects list which Pickford was slow to rectify. In May 1776, after much prevarication, the architect went up to Wirksworth to show, as he put it, that it was 'no Pickpockett Business as represented'.[9]

In a letter to Francis Russell, the Duchy agent in London, he lists his answers to his unnamed accusers, telling us something about the uses to which the building was put. The court room had been let to 'a Company of Stroleing Players', who had 'shamefully broken the stuccoe'. One of the shops had been used by a group of masons working 'on a rough building in the town'. In short he 'never saw a building kept so dirty'.[10] Although the complaints added up to very little, Pickford well understood the principle that attack is the best form of defence when you are in the wrong.

We know from a letter that Pickford wrote to Francis Russell that he was often in the Wirksworth area,[11] and it now seems likely that he was responsible for other work in the town as well as Moot Hall. In the Pickfordian style in Wirksworth is the redbrick, two storey extension to the house in the Market Place which we understand belonged to John Goodwin, the attorney who acted for the Duchy at Moot Hall.

Engraving of Trinity Hospital, Leicester

Plaque from the
Wirksworth Moot Hall

The principal façade, which has recently been restored, has identical Venetian windows to those in No. 44 Friar Gate. Goodwin had an office in Ashbourne and presumably knew Pickford's clients there. The detailing of the Wirksworth house suggests an earlier date than Moot Hall, so it is possible that Goodwin already knew Pickford and persuaded him to submit a tender for Moot Hall after the death of James Eglington.

The second contract Pickford undertook for the Duchy of Lancaster, the Trinity Hospital in the Newarke at Leicester, came through his contact at Wirksworth. By 1775 the building, a fourteenth-century foundation, was badly in need of restoration. The scheme that Pickford proposed and carried out would not have met with the approval of modern conservationists. It was so drastic that even his contemporaries complained, but only on the grounds of utility, certainly not out of concern for the fabric of a medieval building.

The original hospital was an aisled hall, seventeen bays long, with a chapel at one end. There were no clerestory windows so the interior must have been ill lit. Pickford's proposal of February 1776 was to demolish the south aisle and to make the internal arcade the external wall.[12] This he constructed out of brickwork which he later 'frosted', presumably to match the existing stonework. This allowed direct light into the central nave which he formed into two storeys, men on the ground floor and women on the first. The wards were then divided into separate 'cells' to give greater privacy and warmth. Modern inmates would no doubt look askance at such accommodation, but it cannot be denied it was a considerable improvement on what had been thought sufficient in medieval times.

From first to last Trinity Hospital was an ill-fated operation that attracted nothing but hostile criticism for the architect, most of which we now know to have been unfounded. Politics were at the root of the problem, but that does not excuse John Throsby's outrageous attack on Pickford, which he was still pursuing nine years after the architect's death.

In his description of Trinity Hospital published in 1791, Throsby tells us that it was:

Rebuilt at the expense of George the Third . . . It disgraces Royalty. It should say mutilated, patched and cobbled up by and for the profit of —— architect . . . The builder . . . patched up the building in a way most conducive to his own interest, sold much of the timber and lead estimated at £1200 . . . it is now generally believed he cleared upwards of £1000 by the job, when the estimate was only about £400.[13]

How Pickford must have wished these accusations were true. If Throsby had consulted the contract instead of listening to malicious gossip he would have had a different story to tell. The truth is, Pickford had undertaken to do the work for £1,611, of which £896 was to be recovered from the sale of lead and old materials, leaving a balance of £715 to be paid by the Duchy.[14]

Judging from the correspondence it would seem that most of Pickford's problems were caused by his own workmen cheating him as soon as his back was turned. In one instance, Thomas Richardson, the Duchy surveyor, caught the joiners making the windows with rotten timber having previously sold the new oak issued to them for the job.[15] Probably the workmen had been recruited locally and felt no loyalty to their employer, but it does illustrate the problems of control an architect had when the contract he was trying to supervise was the better part of a day's ride away.

As the job progressed the relationship between Pickford and Richardson grew worse. Francis Russell was very concerned and wrote Pickford a letter of great diplomatic skill, which is worth quoting at length:

Your great readiness to accommodate and correct every Error in your workmen bespeaks you to be that fair upright Man I ever took you for. The objects of Mr Richardson's complaints are but trifles in comparison with the work and I wish you would comply with his desires, for when you know him as well as I do you will find him as faithful and honourable as honesty can make a Man. And I am sure when you meet you will talk over matters cooly and deliberately and everything will go right. . . . I assure you I am truly concerned to find you have not made a better bargain for yourself. It will be impossible for you barely upon your own suggestion to get any extra allowances for the badness of the old materials and the badness of the market for lead. But on a proper certificate from Mr Richardson you will have every attention shown to that consideration. And therefore you must on no account suffer your men to do things cheaply and ill because you have not a better prospect of gain. I assure you Mr Richardson highly approves of every part of your plan and will approve of the work too if it is done as it ought to be.[16]

As the work was done in response to a petition drawn up by the inmates of the hospital, it is interesting to find in the archive another petition complaining about the work after it was finished. The paupers, or some old soldier in their ranks, certainly knew a thing or two about drafting petitions. Their interlocutor, a Mr King, seems to have been at his wits end:

I have Drawn myself into a fine scrape by Petitioning the Chancellor for the poor to have the Hospital rebuilt. They now begin to curse me and every other person that advised them to sett their Hands to a Petition. And say they shall all be starved to death for the want of fireplaces. As to the Common Kitchen Fire it will not serve them all for want of room, and in case there was more room it would not be sufficient to warm half of the Poor, the Allowance of Coals being scarcely enough to Cook their Victuals.
   They say further if they were ever so religiously inclined, for want of light they shall not be able to read a chapter in the Bible. And if death should happen to seize some of them in their Houses, who are corpulent, which is very likely to be the case, it will be impossible for their Bodies to be got out without being Mangled, the door cases being so very Narrow they will not be able to get out while living without assistance.[17]

It is good to know that some attention was paid to the poor, as later there was much discussion about the number of fireplaces and the doors to the compartments. Additional light was provided by casements over the doorways, which also helped to control the draughts. To the modern mind these matters seem to be of little importance compared with the sanitary arrangements which were not a source of complaint. Even the new design only allowed for a row of bucket closets in a dismal room off the end of each ward.

Trinity Hospital, Leicester

Of the original building the stone arches and piers of six bays at the eastern end of the main nave and north aisle were still intact in 1981, but most of the building was taken down for a new road scheme in 1898.[18] The hospital's chapel still stands and retains some of its fourteenth-century windows, though nothing of Pickford's work can be seen today.

CHAPTER THIRTEEN

The Edensor Inn and Other Work for the Duke of Devonshire

It says a lot for Pickford's competence and tact that throughout the 1770s, when political rivalry was exacerbated by the break with the American colonies, he still found constant employment at Chatsworth and Kedleston, the rival centres of political power in Derbyshire. But it was to the 5th Duke of Devonshire that he gave his allegiance, for which he was rewarded with architectural commissions and a place on the Derby Corporation. The principal commission, the Edensor Inn, built in 1776–7, still graces the village today.[1]

Apparently the old inn, which stood by the park gates, was not looked upon with great favour and over the years had acquired the kind of reputation which encouraged the discerning traveller to seek his night's lodging elsewhere. At least two noted visitors recorded their feelings about the place. Arthur Young was of the opinion that the traveller 'will find nothing here but dirt and impertinence'.[2] Two years later, in 1773, Dr Johnson stayed there with Mrs Thrale and her family. It was not a happy choice. Genteel middle-aged ladies are not the easiest customers to please, and judging from her comments she was no exception:

> We slept at the wretched inn at Edensor . . . never was there so noisy or disgustful a lodging. I dairst hardly venture to bed there was so many rude drunken people about.[3]

It would seem that not only the building, but the clientèle as well left much to be desired.

The chief reason for the inn being at Edensor was to provide accommodation for visitors who came to see Chatsworth House, so it is not surprising that their complaints soon reached the ears of the Duke himself. The decision to rebuild the inn must have been taken in the autumn or the winter months of 1775–6, when Pickford was fortunately already in the Duke's

The weir in the park, Chatsworth, Derbyshire

employment. The task he had undertaken was a very unusual one, at first sight better suited to an engineer than an architect.

In 1774 the Duke appointed Pickford to supervise the reconstruction of the weir at the southern end of the park, apparently to raise the level of the River Derwent. This was done either to improve the river's appearance as it passed through the park, or to provide a greater head of water for the mill, probably the latter.

There are two accounts for this work: one from the Duke's mason, John Hawksworth, for £167 16s. 7d., and a second from Pickford for £34 13s. 5d., for supervising the masons and making the drawings.[4] Between November

The mill, Chatsworth, Derbyshire

1774 and October 1775 the architect visited the site on nine separate occasions, charging a guinea a day for himself and his horse, plus £6 6s. for his drawings and his expenses at the Edensor Inn.

Clearly the new inn was to be more than just a replacement for the old establishment. A fresh site was chosen outside the park several hundred yards to the north on the road to Baslow, where Pickford erected the present handsome building which has the appearance more of a gentleman's club than the disreputable ale house that Mrs Thrale described.

All of this is clearly shown on a map of 'Edensor Town' dated 1785.[5] This map is of importance because it shows the village at an intermediate stage of development after Capability Brown had removed the High Street to improve the view from the house, but before Joseph Paxton had swept away the old village to make way for his model township in 1837–9.

Superimposed on this map, presumably by Paxton or one of his assistants, is the line of new road which formed part of this redevelopment. Nothing was spared. On each side of the village street the old houses are marked with crosses, like so many dead elms waiting to be felled.

The Edensor Inn, Chatsworth, Derbyshire

The Edensor Inn was more fortunate. Situated away from the old village and the duke's gaze, it was not only spared, but enhanced with a new carriage sweep, where formerly it had stood hard by the road. This is not to say that it had escaped entirely unscathed. Already in its first fifty years of life the improvers had been at work. The substantial *porte-cochère* we see today had been added, and the redbrick stuccoed over. The exact date for these alterations is not known, but Stephen Glover writing about 1829 has an illustration in his *Peak Guide* showing the *porte-cochère* and what he calls 'the stone front'.[6] Happily, the stucco has now been removed to show the brickwork as the architect intended.

Pickford presented two account books for building the new inn. These covered the years 1776–7, and itemized the total cost at £2,551 16s. 3d.[7] The contract was co-ordinated by Pickford's foreman, Richard Fletcher, but the building work was mainly carried out by the Duke's craftsmen working with local materials. Fletcher was paid 3s. 6d. a day 'for looking after the business' from November 1776 to August 1777. There is no separate account paying Pickford for preparing the drawings, but this is to be expected as he took his payment out of the profits of the building.

Apart from the *porte-cochère* mentioned above, the main front facing the road

The *porte-cochère*, the
Edensor Inn, Chatsworth

is still more or less as Pickford designed it. A ballroom was added to the north side in the early years of this century, but it does not affect the basic design.

None of Pickford's drawings has survived, but the accounts describe the original door surround carved by the local mason, John Hawksworth. It had a fluted frieze with moulded caps and columns. Above the door were three stags' heads, the Cavendish Arms, carved by Pickford's Derby associate, George Moneypenny, for £6 6s. We presume these are the same stags' heads which are still under the portico today.

The building ceased to be an hotel when it was converted into a hospital during the First World War. Now it is partly offices and partly a club. Very little of the original interior has survived: the fireplaces and the main stone staircase have gone, though the original layout and proportions of the rooms can still be seen.

The accounts give some idea of the internal finishes. Brailsford of Sheffield papered four of the principal rooms. One area, probably the dining room, was decorated with 'crimson and flowered furniture paper'. But as Brailsford's total bill was only £7 16s., the quality of wallpaper he supplied must have been regarded as a cheap substitute for decorative plasterwork. The best alabaster chimney-piece with carved columns was also in the dining room, at a cost of £15 15s., which was the sort of price a country gentleman of modest means would pay for a dignified piece in his dining room.

Pickford's designs are always ingenious, none more so than the Edensor Inn. Here the central body of the building is of three storeys, with two-storey wings attached directly to the main block. The external plan form, though not the elevational treatment, Pickford took from Robert Adam's design for Lansdowne House in Berkeley Square, which a few years previously had provided him with the inspiration for the main front of St Helen's House in Derby.

Though there have been many changes it is possible to reconstruct the original plan. The main reception rooms were in the wings and approached from the centre, a reversal of the usual arrangement in a country house. This would solve Mrs Thrale's problem, as the noisy customers would be confined to the outer rooms, leaving the guests in the central block to sleep in peace.

Philip Melton, the landlord, moved into the new Edensor Inn in August 1777. A month later James Boswell stayed there on a journey to Scotland, making, as he said, 'a considerable detour to view the magnificence of Chatsworth'.[7] Posing as an innocent tourist seeking anecdotes about Dr Johnson, he quizzed Melton about the great man. 'The very jolly landlord' was taken aback by Boswell's ignorance, but humoured him nevertheless: 'Sir,' said he, 'Johnson, the great writer, Oddity, as they call him. He's the greatest writer in England; he writes for the ministry . . . and lets them know whats going on.' Thus ensuring that Philip Melton's name is remembered by posterity.

The Edensor Inn, Chatsworth, Derbyshire

From the start the new Edensor Inn had a better reputation than its predecessor, probably achieved by putting up the price of alcohol, and forcing the locals to go elsewhere for a night out.

By the early nineteenth century the inn had become very respectable. In 1830 Stephen Glover wrote of it:

> It is a comfortable Inn, situate a short distance from the village church, upon the verge of the Chatsworth Park, and near to the lodge. It is built of stone with a handsome portico. In the open area in front of the house grows a beautiful oak tree. Mr Walters, the present occupier, keeps excellent post chaises and horses; and every accommodation and attention is paid by him and his family to those parties who visit his house.[8]

After the Edensor Inn, further work came Pickford's way. The account books show: 'By sundry bills paid to Mr Pickford and others at Chatsworth in 1778–79, £2360.' This figure ties in with a separate account for building 'Mr Wood's house', itemizing payments to John Hawksworth, the mason, and Richard Fletcher, Pickford's foreman, who was present on the site from

23 August 1777 until 1 May 1779, showing that work on the house began directly after the Edensor Inn was finished.[9]

'Mr Wood' was the Reverend John Wood, vicar of Edensor and Chesterfield, and chaplain to the Duke. As Pickford was almost certainly the architect of Swanwick Hall,[10] their family home, built around 1771, it seems likely that Wood was the person who first introduced Pickford to the Duke. His brother Hugh Wood, who resided at Swanwick, was a patron of Joseph Wright, and well known to John Whitehurst and his circle of friends.

Swanwick Hall near Alfreton, now a school, has been drastically altered since John Wood's day, but from what can be seen of the original building it displays all the hallmarks of Pickford's later work. To the Victorians, the aggressively plain, three-storey, redbrick villa must have seemed more like a workhouse than a gentleman's residence, but the scholarly details and excellent proportions stand out against the ill-considered, nineteenth-century additions.

A close study of the Roman Doric door surround on the main front shows that it was carved out of 'rough rock' gritstone from Horsley Castle Quarry at Coxbench,[11] the source for most of the stone for the better quality, ornamental details on Pickford's work. These parts were made at the workshop in Derby, probably during the winter months when work was slack, and later taken 'off the peg' and built in as required. As Pickford designed most of the houses he built, this could easily have been arranged.

The new vicarage Pickford designed for Wood at Chatsworth stood on the site of the old inn by the park gates and is shown in plan form on the 'Edensor Town' map of 1785. This, alas, is the only known representation of the house which was demolished by Paxton as part of the improvements he carried out in 1837–9. The map shows a substantial dwelling asymmetrical in plan with a large semi-circular bay on the south side looking over the park. Thompson describes it as 'a handsome house', and adds that in dry weather the foundations of it can still be traced.[12] As the house stood in such a prominent position it must have been a building of quality, which gives some hope that one day an illustration of it will come to light.

One more building in Chatsworth Park, which belongs to this period and seems to be Pickford's work, is the lodge gate house immediately behind the Edensor Inn. In 1819 a local historian noted:

> . . . it is a neat stone building, but certainly not sufficiently elegant or ornamented to be an appropriate introduction to so magnificent a mansion; the wooden paling which connects the lodge with the park wall, should give place to something more important and better suited to such a scene.[13]

Perhaps he had a point because the gate house was taken out of commission some time in the nineteenth century, when the central archway was filled in to

The gate house, Edensor, Chatsworth, Derbyshire

form a detached dwelling. Pickford would seem to be the obvious choice for architect as building work began in 1779, directly after the vicarage was completed, and it is recorded that John Hawksworth, the mason who had worked for Pickford on the other contracts, was employed there.[14]

It is true that the stonework is simple and unadorned, but it is none the worse for that. Like most of Pickford's later buildings it relies on proportion to achieve an effect. It cannot be denied that it does lack the scale and effect one would expect to find in a building at the entrance to Chatsworth Park, but it is not without dignity and good manners.

We have left until last the one commission outside Chatsworth Park which Pickford received from the Duke. That is the Devonshire Hospital, or almshouse, in Derby, built in 1777 to replace the original building founded by Bess of Hardwick in the sixteenth century. It formerly stood in Full Street, opposite Amen Alley, but was demolished in 1894 to make way for an extension to the municipal baths which was never carried out. Instead, an electricity power station was built on the site, a municipal folly which greatly disfigured the city centre and happily has since been removed.

Given the quantity of unsorted paper at Chatsworth it would be rash to say no building accounts have survived, but one voucher at least connects Pickford with the building. That is an account for the money paid to Pickford in December 1777, for rehousing the inmates during the forty-four weeks the building took to erect. The average allowance of £1 10s. per person, or 8d. a week, suggests they were content with very modest accommodation.[15]

The new layout, with twelve, single-storey cottages grouped around a courtyard and backing on to a garden which ran down to the River Derwent, must have been an improvement on the original building, but it did not meet with everyone's approval. William Hutton was very jaundiced about the project:

> Who dresses a pauper in lace, instead of that modest elegance which ought to have dignified the front. . . . we are treated to an ostentatious display of the Duke's Arms and Crest as the leading objects.[16]

Perhaps Hutton had a point. The grand architectural screen that faced the street certainly had more to do with pride than the comfort of the paupers. The only other contemporary description we have of the building accords very closely with Hutton's view.

In 1782, the year of Pickford's death, a visitor kept a journal of a visit to Derbyshire in which he describes the hospital at some length:

> Near the great church which is much admired are built some almshouses by the Duke of Devonshire. The front has more the appearance of magnificence than charity and opens onto a courtyard surrounded by small apartments. In the middle of this court opposite the entrance a flight of steps leads to the lower rooms which is the only means of communication with the upper chambers. This I believe cannot be but inconvenient to the aged and decrepit. But our surprise at this was much heightened by our enquiries after the objects of this benefaction who scarcely appeared to be under the necessity of claiming such a bounty from age or visible infirmity. We were then informed that their abode was optional and that they had the discretionary powers of letting their apartments or gardens to others. How far this is an abuse of the charity must be determined by the original intention of the founder.[17]

If this account is correct there would seem to have been very little point in rebuilding the Devonshire Hospital, as Hutton assured his readers that the original 'building was of stone which would have stood the blasts for five hundred years to come'.[18] The accommodation was not greatly improved and any credit the Duke might have received for undertaking the work was lost in the ridicule heaped upon the design.

The Devonshire Almshouse, Full Street, Derby

The Duke seems to have been badly advised in the matter, and possibly Pickford lost credit by it as shortly afterwards the plum contract for the Crescent at Buxton was handed to John Carr of York. Carr was the leading architect in the north of England, which is probably why he was preferred, but Pickford's disappointment must have been acute, as the Crescent was the sort of commission he needed to gain a national reputation.

145

CHAPTER FOURTEEN

Ashford Hall and the Work of
George Moneypenny

One of the more intriguing buildings in Derbyshire, which can confidently be attributed to Pickford, is Ashford Hall, in the village of Ashford in the Water. It stands on an elevated position overlooking the River Wye, about two miles north of Bakewell and about four miles from Chatsworth House. Stephen Glover, writing in 1833, said that 'it is an elegant residence . . . surrounded by beautiful plantations overlooking a rich valley and commanding all the diversified and picturesque scenery of that romantic river.'[1] Today the house is little changed, and the situation is still very much as Glover described it.

Nothing is known of the building history of Ashford Hall and there is even some doubt about who built it. The best information we have comes from the Lysons, usually reliable witnesses. Writing in 1817, some forty years after the house was built, they tell us that 'near Ashford is a good house, the property and residence of the late Thomas Barker Esq. and now in the occupation of his widow. It was built by Mr Barker's father.'[2]

John Barker (1731–95), the father of Thomas Barker (1767–1816), was of local descent and, like his grandfather and father before him, agent to the Duke of Rutland. His residence is given in Burke's *Landed Gentry* as The Hall, Bakewell, the house provided by the Duke for his Derbyshire agent. Assuming the Lysons were correct the matter is further complicated by letters in the archives at Chatsworth, dating from the late 1770s and directed to Alexander Barker, the Duke of Devonshire's agent, at Ashford Hall.[3] It is not necessary to go into the ramifications of the Barker family except to say that John and Alexander were near kinsmen, and must have been well known to each other.

A month before he died, in August 1795, John Barker drew up his will which in part explains why Alexander Barker was living in the house. John Barker does not claim to have built Ashford Hall, but he does say that 'for better securing the payments of my said debts . . . legacies and funeral

Ashford Hall, Derbyshire

expenses I do hereby charge my estates purchased by me in the Manor of Ashford and . . . at Coats Park with the payment of the same'.

There were five children in the family: Thomas, John, Robert, Jane and Sarah. Thomas, the eldest son, and John, he appointed as his executors. As he entreated the Duke of Rutland to allow his son John to tenant the house in Bakewell, 'which I now inhabit with the farm and tithes I hold of his Grace', it seems reasonable to suppose that Thomas paid off the legacies to his brothers and sisters and took Ashford Hall for himself.

Pickford's claim to be the architect of Ashford Hall rests mainly on the ornamental detail, in particular the distinctive urn carved on the pediment of the porch, a design associated with Pickford's old colleague, George Moneypenny. As Moneypenny used the design on a number of occasions after the architect's death, we assume that the version at Ashford is the original and was the work of Joseph Pickford.

The five-bay, three-storey façade facing the garden has much in common with St Helen's House in Derby. Like St Helen's the ground-floor windows are set in blind arcades, though at Ashford these windows were enlarged in the nineteenth century to admit more light to the principal rooms. This new arrangement may have improved the interior, but it certainly did nothing to help the proportions of the façade.

147

At the same time as the windows were added, the ground floor was turned about face so that the original carriage front now looks on to the garden. Today the main entrance is reached through the conservatory to the west, leaving the original hallway as a lobby separating the reception rooms from the garden. This lobby is faced with an elegant Ionic door surround, the only ornamental feature on the façade. On the entablature of this porch is a grotesque frieze with a distinctive urn which we believe was designed by Pickford and carved by Moneypenny.

On rising ground to the east of the house is a workman's cottage posing as a garden temple. At a distance it seems to be a building of some refinement, but closer inspection reveals that it was built on the cheap, with plain window surrounds and poor quality ashlar. Of interest are the mason's tooling marks on the face of the ashlar, for these are similar to John Hawksworth's work at Edensor.

The design, reminiscent of the work of William Kent, has a central recessed porch, with a portico, *distyle in antis*, and Venetian and Diocletian windows in the solid walls each side. The capitals of the columns show the cottage to be contemporary with the house. These capitals were of a type derived from the Tower of the Winds in Athens, which means that Pickford probably took the idea from Stuart and Revett's famous volume, *The Antiquities of Athens*,

Detail of the door pediment, Ashford Hall, Ashford in the Water, Derbyshire

Ashford Hall, Ashford in the Water, Derbyshire

published in 1762. The same capitals, derived by the Greeks from an Egyptian form, appear again in the screen in the Hall, and yet again at Pickford's own house in Derby.

The grotesque ornament in the pediment of the garden porch, apart from pointing to a connection with Joseph Pickford and George Moneypenny, also helps to date the house. The idea for the design, with the urn supported on acanthus scrollwork, was probably taken from George Richardson's, *A Book of Ceilings Composed in the Stile of the Antique Grotesque*, published in 1776, to which Pickford was an original subscriber. James Gandon's publication, *A Collection of Friezes, Capitals and Grotesque Ornaments*, which was published two years later, contains similar designs which Pickford might have known.

Garden Cottage, Ashford Hall

Another design featuring grotesque ornament which may have influenced Pickford is an intriguing architectural design in the collection of Joseph Wright's Italian drawings in the Derby Museum. Howard Colvin has pointed out that it is related to a set of designs for a grand 'Roman House' which the French architect Charles Louis Clerisseau made for the Empress Catherine of Russia in 1773, the same year Joseph Wright painted for the Empress *An Iron Forge Viewed from Without*. The house was never built, but the original drawings, like Wright's painting, are now at the Hermitage in St Petersburg.

There is no lettering on the drawing in the Wright collection, except a scale in feet and inches, which suggests that it is a copy made by an English draughtsman. We know that Robert Adam engaged Clerisseau in Florence in 1754,[5] and that three years later he accompanied Adam to Dalmatia where they explored and measured the ruins of the Roman Palace of Diocletian at Split, the subject of Adam's first great publication in 1764.

Joseph Wright himself went to Italy in October 1773, and was in Rome in

February 1774 when he heard that the empress had decided to take his picture.[6] It now seems almost certain that he met Clérisseau at this time and acquired the drawing, though for what purpose we can only guess. As he brought it back to Derby with him it is highly likely that he showed it to Pickford as an example of a neo-classical design by a respected master.

Most of the ideas contained in Clérisseau's drawing were part of the neo-classical vocabulary available to any architect, but what appears to be unique to the design in the frieze at Ashford is the urn with handles in the form of serpents. The original idea seems to have been taken from James Gibbs' *Book of Architecture*. Gibbs illustrates an urn with serpent handles as one of '54 draughts of vases in the antique manner made for several persons at different times'. But it is difficult to see how such an object could be made in three dimensions as the handles would be far too fragile for practical use.

Moneypenny used it only in bas-relief, but there is a recorded example of a similar thing cast in metal. John Vardy in his volume, *Some Designs of Mr Inigo Jones and Mr William Kent*, published in 1744, shows a 'Gold Cup for Colonel Pelham' with serpent handles.

Used symbolically the urn in classical times signified death, as it was derived from the cinerary urn in which the ancients preserved the ashes of the dead, a practice which continued until Christianity was generally adopted in the Roman world. To the Romans the urn was also a symbol of fate, as it was used in elections as a receptacle for voting tablets. The serpent to the Romans was associated with immortality and healing. Aesculapius, the God of Medicine, was usually depicted carrying a staff entwined with a serpent.

Apart from the pediment at Ashford, there are eight other examples of the urn with serpent handles in the Derby area, all of which we associate with Pickford or Moneypenny: two on chimney-pieces and six on memorial plaques.

First the two examples on chimney-pieces as we are less certain about their date. Of these only one is still *in situ*, that is at Staunton Harold Hall, Leicestershire, which was built to the designs of the owner, Washington Shirley, 5th Earl Ferrers, between 1762 and 1775.[7] Pickford was well known to Ferrers and he almost certainly designed this chimney-piece as well as others in the house. There is a payment in the records of 1772 of £5 5s. to George Moneypenny, 'on account',[8] but it is not known if this was for the chimney-piece.

A second chimney-piece with a similar plaque, though in this case the urn rests on a foliate base like the one over the door at Ashford in the Water, was formerly at Egginton Hall, Derbyshire, until the house was demolished after the Second World War. Samuel Wyatt remodelled the house for Sir Edward Every in 1782,[9] and his account book shows that George Moneypenny was

Detail of the chimney-piece, Staunton Harold Hall

responsible for the carving. In April 1782 he was paid £31 7s. for the 'Door case for the new front door',[10] and there are several other payments to him on account, but again no specific reference to the chimney-piece. However, it is possible that Sir Edward purchased the chimney-piece at the sale following Pickford's death in July 1782, which Moneypenny organized.[11]

This sale by auction of Pickford's stock-in-trade in September 1782 is the only glimpse we have into the sculptural side of his business. The auction, which ran over two days, was advertised in the *Derby Mercury*. The second day was reserved for the sale of the marble statuary:

> Likewise on Tuesday the 3rd of September, will be Sold by Auction, several Grand Marble Chimney Pieces, and an assortment of Statuary, Sianah, [Siena] Dove and White and Vein Marble . . . Printed catalogues to be had of the Auctioneer and at Mr Moneypenny's, Nun's Green, who will show the Goods until the Day of the Sale.

There is no saying who purchased these wares, except that Moneypenny himself was well positioned to do so, in particular the stock of marble which the gentry would not have wanted. Of the marble described, the white Carrara and the yellow Siena were commonplace in Pickford's chimney-

The chimney-piece at Egginton Hall, Derbyshire

pieces, and after Pickford's death Moneypenny continued to use his ideas, almost without change, right up to his own demise in October 1807.

Listed below are the monuments we attribute to George Moneypenny which we shall consider in chronological order:

1. Ashbourne church, Derbys. Monument to Mr Brian Hodgson, died 13 December 1781.

Hodgson was well known to Pickford through the Derby Assembly Rooms and his house in Ashbourne. Of this group, this is the only one to be erected in

153

In Memory of
Mr BRIAN HODGSON late of this Town
He was in Principle and in Practice,
An honest Man and a sincere Christian.
He died December 18. 1781. Aged 75.
ELIZABETH RELICT OF THE ABOVE,
DIED NOV 29 1808 AGED 90.

The Hodgson Memorial,
Ashbourne church, Ashbourne

Pickford's lifetime, and though it shares all the design characteristics of the others it does not have the serpent handles.

2. Bradbourne church, Derbys. Monument to Mrs Sarah Buckston, wife of Mr George Buckston of Bradbourne Hall, died 9 February 1793.

We are told that 'Her surviving daughter caused this monument to be erected.' This lady, Martha Buckston, married first, Dr John Beridge of Derby in 1775 and second, the Revd T.F. Twigge in 1792. Twigge was the vicar of Tickhill, Yorkshire but resided with his wife in St Werburgh's parish, Derby, where they moved in the same circle as Joseph Wright and Mrs Pickford. Martha Twigge died at Bakewell in 1827, and is commemorated in the parish church with a plaque by Joseph Hall of Derby.

3. Mayfield church, Staffs. Monument to Thomas Ley Esq. of Middle Mayfield, Barrister at Law, died 22 March 1795, and his wife Susanna, died 26 October 1800.

On this plaque the urn is partially draped with only one handle showing. The

Monument to Sarah Buckston, Bradbourne
church, Derbyshire

Design for a monument for Joseph Wright,
St Alkmund's church, Derby

Ley family lived at Mayfield Hall which was extended about 1790 in a plain, late Georgian design, in the style of Thomas Gardner of Uttoxeter, Pickford's former assistant (see below).

   4. St Alkmund's church, Derby. Monument to Joseph Wright, died 29 August 1797.

This plaque disappeared when St Alkmund's was demolished in the nineteenth century and is known today only from a drawing.[12] Although the urn is identical to the others the surround to the plaque is different.

   5. Wirksworth church, Derbys. Monument to Francis Hurt, of Alderwasley Hall, died 5 January 1801.

This plaque is similar to the one in Mayfield church, partially draped with only one handle showing.

   6. & 7. Uttoxeter church, Staffs. Monuments to Thomas Gardner, architect, died 4 October 1804, and Mary Gardner, his wife, died 1 September 1806.

These two monuments are identical and probably came from Gardner's stock.

   Thomas Gardner advertised in the *Derby Mercury* from time to time offering his services as an architect and surveyor. In addition he also offered to supply chimney-pieces and monuments. As he was a joiner by trade it seems likely that he sublet this work to Moneypenny. After Pickford's death Gardner took on many of his old workmen, and he also appears to have known Pickford's subcontractors and suppliers.

   As Moneypenny never signed his monuments all that can be said for certain is that the examples cited above were erected in his lifetime. It is likely that other similar plaques unknown to us still adorn the walls of parish churches in the midland counties, but it is doubtful if they will add much more to our knowledge of Pickford, Moneypenny and their circle of clients.

   As no proof positive exists to connect Pickford and Moneypenny with the serpent-handled urn, it is necessary to set down the few facts we do know about their relationship so that the reader can judge for himself. Neither Moneypenny nor his wife were Derby people. There is no record of their presence in the town before September 1766, when they baptized their daughter Anne at St Werburgh's church.[13] George Moneypenny was then twenty-six years old, a time-served craftsman, and apparently a stranger to the district, though he must have had some business contacts, otherwise necessity would have forced him to advertise his services. Two years later, in July 1768, a

Monument to Thomas Gardner, Uttoxeter
church, Staffordshire

Monument to Francis Hurt, Wirksworth
church, Derbyshire

157

son was also taken to the font in St Werburgh's. George Moneypenny junior, who later became a successful London architect and is noticed separately.

It is tempting to believe that it was Pickford who brought Moneypenny to the town. This may have been the case, but there is no documentary evidence to connect the two before 1776, when Moneypenny was working at Kedleston Hall under Pickford's direction.[14] It cannot even be claimed that Pickford introduced him to Kedleston as Moneypenny was carving the *paterae* on the Boat House before Pickford was appointed.

At Kedleston Moneypenny was largely responsible for the carving in the Hall, apparently in wood as well as stone, as the accounts mention: the base and sub-base mouldings, the saloon door, the side doors to the Hall, and the frames to the paintings in the Hall. Pickford was also responsible for fluting the alabaster columns which he entrusted to another mason, suggesting that he reserved Moneypenny for the more exacting work.

An authority on the paintings of Joseph Wright has recently stated that the frame to the portrait of the Pickford children is one of the finest to be associated with his work. She goes on to say that 'closer inspection shows it to be entirely hand carved. No frame like it has yet been recorded.'[15] The writer suggests that the frame was designed by Pickford and carved by Moneypenny. As the portrait dates from the years 1777–9, she is almost certainly correct.

The stags' heads carved for the Edensor Inn,[16] and the sale of Pickford's stock previously mentioned are the only other recorded examples of their association. We know that Moneypenny worked close to Pickford on Nun's Green, but they were not partners in the formal sense, sharing the profits of a joint business. However, it is likely that they had some sort of understanding and mutual regard for each other, probably based on Moneypenny's ability to produce work of the desired standard.

What little we know about Moneypenny's private life we owe to the *Derby Mercury*. If obituaries are to be believed then George and his wife had a good marriage, marred only by Mary's health. She died in August 1803.

> On the 24th inst. after a severe and heavy bodily affliction of eight years which she bore with Christian patience, truly regretted by her family and friends, Mrs Mary Moneypenny, wife of Mr G. Moneypenny of this town, sculptor.[17]

George outlived his wife by four years and died in October 1807. His notice is even more perfunctory:

> On Tuesday last, aged 69, Mr George Moneypenny of this place, sculptor.[18]

As funerary monuments were an important part of his business, it is unfortunate that St Alkmund's church in Derby, where Moneypenny and his wife were buried, was demolished in 1841, and none of his work there has survived. That is apart from the drawing of the plaque to Joseph Wright.

It is tempting to believe that Pickford had a part in setting George Moneypenny junior on the road to becoming an architect, but as he was only fourteen years old when Pickford died this must be doubted. Clearly he was apprenticed to his father as the Derby Directory of 1792, when the son was twenty-four, lists them both as carvers.[19]

However, this is not the complete story, as on 11 December 1793, the *Derby Mercury* records:

> Mr Bonomi . . . has presented to the R.A. sketches of sectional perspective views . . . of the Vatican and Basilica of St Peter in Rome and employed the ingenious architect and draughtsman Mr G. Moneypenny jnr. of this town to make complete finished copies of the same, which will be shown in the public exhibition . . . and afterwards deposited in . . . the British Museum.

It is not known if Moneypenny had studied under Joseph Bonomi (1739–1808), but his first recorded building was the Leicester County Gaol, built between 1790 and 1792.[20] He later specialized in such buildings, but at Leicester, where he was the contractor as well as architect, Moneypenny got into financial difficulties and was one of the first to be imprisoned for debt in his own gaol.[21]

At this early date he must have worked from Derby, but shortly afterwards he moved to London where he established a national reputation. There are no recorded buildings by him in Derby, but in 1804 he was one of the unsuccessful architects who submitted designs for the new Derbyshire General Infirmary.[22]

Notes

Chapter 1

1. Colvin, H.M., *Biographical Dictionary of British Architects, 1660–1840*, London 1978, 747–53.
2. Ibid.
3. Bishop's Transcripts, Herefordshire CRO.
4. Hearth Tax Returns, Herefordshire CRO.
5. Marriage Licenses, Worcestershire CRO.
6. Ibid.
7. Field, W., *History of Warwick*, 1815, 374.
8. Colvin, op. cit., 69.
9. Parish Register, info. A. Gomme.
10. Colvin, op. cit., 763–4.
11. Marriage Licenses, Worcestershire CRO.
12. Harris, J., *Sir William Chambers*, London, 1970.
13. Croome Court building accounts, info. H. Colvin.
14. Lothian archive, Melbourne Hall.
15. Staffordshire CRO., D593/D/16/2/4/20.
16. Gomme, A., 'Catton Hall', in *The Country Seat*, ed. Colvin, H. and Harris, J., 1970, 157–63.
17. Wills and Administrations, 1730, Worcestershire CRO.
18. Leigh Papers, Stoneleigh, No. 38f. Shakespeare's Birthplace Trust RO, Stratford.
19. Bishop's Transcripts, Ashow, Warwicks., Joint Record Office, Lichfield.
20. Wills, 1742, Joint Record Office, Lichfield.
21. Wills, 1748, Worcestershire CRO.
22. Gunnis, R., *Dictionary of British Sculptors, 1660–1851*, London, 1953, 183.
23. Ibid.
24. Barlaston, Wedgwood Museum, Wedgwood to Cox, 30 April 1768.
25. London rate books.
26. Ibid.
27. Sir John's Soane's Museum, 39B.
28. Holkham accounts, info. L. Harris.
29. Colvin, H. (ed.), *History of the King's Works*, V, 438.
30. Ibid. Works, 6/63, 26 April, 1 and 8 May, 1750.
31. Willis, R. and Clarke, J., *The Architectural History of the University of Cambridge*, 3 vols. III, 63–68.
32. DNB.
33. *Architectural History*, XXV, 1982, 27.
34. PRO Prob. II, Lynch, 478.
35. Colvin, op. cit., 19.

Chapter 2

1. Wiltshire CRO, Burdett Papers, Accounts A1/1.
2. Colvin, op. cit., 421.
3. Holkham accounts, info. L. Harris.
4. Derbyshire CRO, account book signed by Pickford among the Strutt papers.
5. On the strength of Pickford's friendship with Wright (Mozley, T., *Reminiscences*, 1.65) and attested as a friend of Burdett in Egerton, J., *Wright of Derby* (London, 1990), 87–91.
6. Mozley, loc. cit.
7. Ibid.
8. Egerton, J, catalogue, Wright of Derby exhibition, Tate Gallery, London (1990), 216–7.
9. Nicholson, B., *Joseph Wright, Painter of Light*, 2 vols. (London, 1968), 1.36. Catalogue 156; 11. plate 82.
10. Ibid.
11. Public Records Office, Kew, PRO IR 1/22.
12. Nicolson, op. cit., 1.2.
13. Meaby, K.T. (ed.), *Nottingham County Records of the Eighteenth Century* (1947) 54.
14. Gandon, J. (ed), *Vitruvius Britannicus*, vol. V. (London, 1771), pp. 31–5 and 90–3.
15. Colvin, op. cit., 781–2.
16. University Library Keele, Mottershaw to Wedgwood, 31141/11.
17. Nicolson, op. cit., 1.12, n.1.
18. Ibid.
19. Derby Museum, Wright drawings collection.
20. Hutton, C., *Obituary of John Whitehurst*, FRS (London, 1791).
21. Craven, M., *The Derby Town House* (Derby, 1978), 84–5.
22. Darwin, E., *The Economy of Vegetation* (1791), 11, 17n.
23. King-Hele, D., *Doctor of Revolution* (London, 1977), 14, 60–1.
24. Birmingham Reference Library, Boulton collection, letters, Whitehurst to Boulton, 30/10/1775, and 12/7/1776.
25. PRO Patent, 15/11/1774.
26. Nottingham University Library, Newcastle papers, accounts.
27. Hutton, op. cit., 15.
28. Birmingham Reference Library, Boulton collection, letter Pickford to Boulton, 5/12/1760.
29. Birmingham Reference Library, notes taken by the Revd B. Clarke from St Mary's minute book, now lost.
30. Meteyard, E., *The Life of Josiah Wedgwood*, 2 vols., 1865.
31. Essex CRO copy of the will of the Revd Peter Perez, vicar of Eastwood, dated 17/4/1748, proved 12/11/1750 (Essex CRO 366 Greenly); baptism, ibid., T/A 38/55.
32. Nicolson, op. cit., 1.2.
33. I am indebted to Mr Maxwell Craven of the Derby Museum for this suggestion.
34. On the existence of the house by 1768, see a painting in the Derby Museum of it, 'after an original by P.P. Burdett' Goodey No. 372. The address given for Burdett in an advertisement in the *Derby Mercury* (20/6/1766) leaves little doubt of the identification.
35. Nicolson, op. cit., 1.2.
36. DNB (combined edition, 2 vols. Oxford, 1975), 1.523.
37. Derby Local Studies Library, a pamphlet entitled: 'A List of the Honorary Burgesses of the Borough of Derby made since the Last Election', dated Derby 7 Sept. 1776.
38. Derby Local Studies Library, Derby Burgess Rolls, 31/5/1778.
39. Kedleston archives, info. Mr L. Harris.

40. I am indebted to Mr Maxwell Craven of the Derby Museum for this information.
41. I am indebted to the Keeper of the Records of the Grand Lodge of England, and to Mr John Williams for this information.
42. This information emerges from a long series of advertisements in the *Derby Mercury*, Derby Local Studies Library.
43. Derby Rate Book (nd) in Derby Museum.
44. *Derby Mercury*, 2/4/1779; *London Gazette*, 11961 (23-27/3/1779).
45. *Derbyshire Advertiser*, 29/10/1915.
46. Derbyshire CRO D769/29 and P46.
47. *Derby Mercury*, obituary, 17/7/1815.
48. Mozley, loc. cit.
49. *Architectural History*.
50. Pevsner, Sir N., *Derbyshire* (1st edn. London 1953), 108.
51. *Derby Mercury*, obituary, 11/7/1782.
52. Ibid., 22/8/1782.

Chapter 3

1. University of Keele Sneyd Papers, Pickfords proposals, Aug. 1761.
2. Colvin, op. cit., 243.
3. University of Keele Sneyd Papers.
4. Derbyshire CRO Account Book.
5. Barlaston, Wedgwood Museum, Wedgwood to Bentley.
6. *Derby Mercury*, obituary 11/7/1782.

Chapter 4

1. Colvin, op. cit., 420.
2. Wiltshire CRO Burdett Papers.
3. *Vitruvius Britannicus*, vol. V., 1771.
4. Craven, M.A.J.B., *The Derbyshire Country House*, Derby (1991), pp. 90–2.
5. *Vitruvius Britannicus*, vol. V. 1771.
6. Byng, Hon. J., *The Torrington Diaries*, Andrews, C. (ed.), London, 1935.
7. Byng, op. cit.
8. Ibid.
9. Wooley, W., *History of Derbyshire*, and Glover, C., Riden, P., Derbys. Records Soc. vol. 6, 1981, 143.
10. Information courtesy Dr K. Goodway, of Keele University.
11. Wiltshire CRO Burdett Papers, Accts 9 Feb. 1759, 'Pd Mr Hiorns a bill for Knowlhills £23.'
12. Craven, op. cit., pp. 24–5.
13. Birmingham Reference Library, Boulton collection, Pickford to Boulton, 6 Dec. 1760.
14. Colvin, op. cit., 520.
15. Ibid., 936.
16. Wenman Coke was still listed by Pickford as his arbiter in 1776 on his contract with the Duchy of Lancaster at Leicester Trinity Hospital.
17. University Library Keele, Sneyd Papers, Pickford to Sneyd 13 May 1762.

18. White, W., *Directory of Staffordshire* (Sheffield, 1834), p. 643.
19. University Library Keele, Sneyd Papers, Pickford's proposals, August 1761.
20. Ibid.
21. Derbys. CRO Drawings among the Harpur Crewe Archives, info. about discovery from Mr H. Colvin.
22. Colvin, op. cit.
23. Derbys. CRO Harpur Crewe Archives, D23 75M 184/4.
24. Derbys. CRO Harpur Crewe Archives.
25. PRO Duchy of Lancaster Archive, 42/175.
26. Nottingham University Library, MAB 115.
27. Wittkower, R., *Palladio and English Palladianism*, London, 1947.

Chapter 5

1. Girouard, M., *Country Life*, 2/10/1986, p. 1050.
2. Colvin, op. cit., 131.
3. Defoe, *A Tour Through the Whole Island of Great Britain*, ed. Rogers, P. (London, 1986), 170.
4. Glover, S., *A History and Gazetteer of the County of Derby* (Derby 1st edition, 1829/31), 11.427.
5. Signboard preserved in the Derby Museum.
6. Girouard, M., op. cit.
7. Derbyshire CRO, DRO 239/098.
8. Colvin, op. cit., 431.
9. Derbyshire CRO, account book, op. cit.
10. Colvin, op. cit., 413.
11. Ibid., 733.
12. Nicolson, B., op. cit., 1., 105–6.
13. *Derby Mercury*, 30 July 1771.
14. Wittkower, R., *Palladio and English Palladianism* (London, 1974), 136.
15. Gunnis, op. cit., 314.
16. Craven, M., *The Illustrated History of Derby* (Derby, 1988), 133; James Denstone also succeeded Samuel Wyatt as clerk of works at Kedleston Hall, but was later dismissed by Lord Scarsdale for his 'whiggish' opinions.

Chapter 6

1. Boswell, J., *Life of Samuel Johnson, The World's Classics*, Oxford University Press, 1360–1, Johnson arrived in Ashbourne 20 July 1784.
2. King-Hele, op. cit., 62.
3. Seward, A., *Memoirs of the Life of Dr Johnson* (1804), 99–100.
4. Egerton, J., op. cit., 117.
5. At Shirley.
6. Craven, M. and Stanley, M., *The Derbyshire Country House*, 2 vols. (Matlock, 1982 and 1984), 11. 14.
7. Derbyshire Record Office, DRO 239/098.
8. DAJ. XXX (1910) 23–44.
9. *Country Life*, 28/3/1968.
10. Hodgson, DAJ. LX (1939) 16–17.
11. See note 7.
12. I am indebted to Mr Maxwell Craven for this information.
13. Derbyshire Record Office, Turbutt Papers, 37M P10.

14. Worsley, G., in *Architectural History*, XXXIII (1990), 60–74.

15. Bearman R., 'A Lost Warwickshire Country House, Stivichall Hall', in *Warwickshire History* (9), 1970.

16. Keele University, Sneyd Papers, letter from Pickford to Ralph Sneyd, 13/5/1762.

17. I am indebted to Michael Stanley for this information.

18. Ashbourne, *A Georgian Country Town*, ed. Henstock, A., Nottingham, 1989, vol. 1, 33.

19. DAJ. LX (1939), 12–14.

20. Broadley, A.M., *Dr Johnson and Mrs Thrale*, London, 1910, 164.

21. Chapman, R.W., *Letters of Dr Johnson*, 3 vols., Oxford, 1963, 1/171.

22. Boswell, op. cit.

23. DNB, op. cit., 1.695, and Boswell, op. cit.

24. *The History of Parliament, The House of Commons, 1754–90*, by Sir Lewis Namier and Sir John Brooke (HM Stationery), vol. II, Members A–J, 429.

25. Ibid.

26. Boswell, op. cit.

27. Namier and Brooke, op. cit., vol. II, 430.

28. Boswell, op. cit.

29. Craven, op. cit., 89–93.

30. Framed bill at Tissington Hall.

31. Gunnis, op. cit., 89–93.

32. For information on the building stone I am indebted to Mr Michael Stanley.

33. DNB, op. cit.

34. Deeds No. 44 Friar Gate, Derby. Private Collection.

35. Craven and Stanley, op. cit., 11.19.

36. Ashbourne, op. cit., 21.

37. Christian, R., *The Butterley Co.*, London, 1990.

38. Document in the possession of Lloyd's Bank, Ashbourne.

Chapter 7

1. For the notes on Selva's life and details of his diary I am indebted to Mr P. DuPrey, and his leaflet 'Gianantonio Selva in England', reprinted from *Architectural History*, vol. 25, 1982.

2. Translation kindly supplied by Mr DuPrey.

3. DuPrey, op. cit., 22.

4. Ibid., 23

5. Info. Mr Max Craven.

6. Barlaston, Wedgwood Museum, letter Wedgwood to Bentley, Dec. 1767.

7. Colvin, op. cit., 51.

8. Adam, Robert and James, *Works in architecture*, 1773.

9. DNB, op. cit.

10. Letter J. Whitehurst to B. Franklyn, 21 May 1772. Info. Mr Max Craven.

11. Craven, M. and Stanley, M., *Derbyshire Country House*, Matlock, 1984, 33.

12. *Derby Mercury*.

13. Wiltshire CRO, Burdett Papers, accounts.

14. Barlaston, op. cit., Wedgwood to Bentley, 31 Dec. 1767.

15. Hutton, W., *History of Derby*, London, 1791, 29–30.

16. Craven, M., *The Derby Town House*, Derby, 1987, 95.

17. *Derby Mercury*, 29 May 1767.

18. Derby Directories, and info. from Sister Imelda, of the Order of Mercy.

19. Barlaston, op. cit., Wedgwood to Bentley, 15 Sept. 1768.

20. Gomme, A., *Catton Hall in the Country Seat*, ed. Colvin, H.M. and Harris, J. 1970, 157–63.
21. Sheppard, E.C., *The Tower and Bells of Solihull Church*, 1950, 20.
22. Colvin, op. cit., 635.

Chapter 8

1. Barlaston, Wedgwood Museum, letter, Wedgwood to Bentley, Dec. 1767.
2. Wedgwood, Barbara and Hensleigh, *The Wedgwood Circle 1730–1897*, 1980, 20.
3. Wedgwood, op. cit.
4. Ibid., 25–6.
5. Ibid.
6. King-Hele, D., *Doctor of Revolution*, London, 1977, 260.
7. Barlaston, op. cit., Wedgwood to Bentley, 15 March 1768.
8. Ibid., July 1767.
9. Ibid., 30 Nov. 1767.
10. Ibid., Dec. 1767.
11. Ibid., 16 Jan. 1768.
12. Ibid., 30 March 1768.
13. Lichfield Joint Records Office, Bishop's Transcripts, St Werburgh's, Derby.
14. Wedgwood, op. cit., 38.
15. Barlaston, op. cit., Wedgwood to Bentley, 8 Sept. 1768.
16. Ibid., 15 Sept. 1768.
17. Meteyard, E., *The Life of Josiah Wedgwood*, 2 vols., 1865.
18. Colvin, op. cit., 635.
19. Barlaston, op. cit., Wedgwood to Bentley, 23 Jan. 1768.
20. I am obliged to Dr K. Goodway of Keele University for this information.
21. Meteyard, op. cit., 128.
22. Ibid.
23. Byng, op. cit.
24. Barlaston, op. cit., Wedgwood to Bentley, Nov. 1768.
25. Wedgwood, op. cit., 42.
26. Barlaston, op. cit., Wedgwood to Bentley, 3 Jan. 1768.
27. Ibid., 30 April 1768.
28. Wedgwood in London, Catalogue to the 225th Anniversary Exhibition, 1759–1984, 8.
29. Keele University, letter, Pickford to Wedgwood, 18 Dec. 1771.
30. Barlaston, op. cit., Wedgwood to Bentley, 20 June 1768.
31. Ibid., 13 April 1772.

Chapter 9

1. Byng, op. cit.
2. Deeds in private collection.
3. Deeds in Derby Museum.
4. Mozley, T., *Reminiscences*, 1882, 1 chapter 9.
5. Deeds in Derby Museum.
6. For this information I am indebted to Mr John Williams, a student of Freemasonry.
7. Bemrose, W., *The Life and Works of Joseph Wright*, Derby, 1855.
8. *Derby Mercury*.
9. Deeds in Derby Museum.
10. Ibid.

11. Ibid.
12. Ibid.
13. Deeds in private collection.
14. *Derby Mercury*.
15. Deeds in private collection.
16. Ibid.
17. Phillips, Sir R., *A Personal Tour through the U.K.*, vol. 2, Derby and Notts., London, 1828, 109.

Chapter 10

1. Harrowby Mss., Sandon Hall, Staffs.
2. Harris, J.
3. Barlaston, Wedgwood collection.
4. Autobiography of Dudley, 1st Earl of Harrowby, printed privately, 1891, 12.
5. Dudley, loc. cit., 13.
6. Byng, op. cit.
7. I am obliged to Dr Keith Goodway for this information.
8. Another is in the collections of Derby Museum.
9. Holkham Park, *Its Development Over Three Centuries*, 1983, Jarrold Publications. Drawing by Brettingham, of Kent's North Lodge (no longer standing).
10. Vardy, J., *Some Designs of Mr Inigo Jones and Mr William Kent* (1744), plate 50.
11. Colvin, op. cit., 147 and 425. Brown and Holland worked at Trentham 1775–8.
12. Lothian archives, Melbourne Hall, accounts, 1773.
13. Lothian archives, op. cit., letter from Viscount Melbourne to his agent, Fox, at Melbourne, dated 17 Oct. 1770.
14. Lothian archives, accounts, 1773, Pickford was paid £633 6s. 9d. for his work on the roof.
15. History of Leicestershire, vol. III, pt. 2.
16. PRO, Duchy of Lancaster MSS.
17. Throsby, J., *Select Views in Leicestershire . . . Containing seats of the Nobility and Gentry, Town Views and Ruins*, Leicester (1789).

Chapter 11

1. Reprinted in the *Derby Mercury*, 2 Sept. 1774.
2.   Notes taken from the minute book by the Revd Basil Clarke, now in the collection of the Birmingham Public Libraries.
3. Gill, C., History of Birmingham, Oxford University Press, 1952.
4. Colvin, op. cit., 304 Roger Eyken, architect.
5. Clarke, op. cit.
6. Ibid.
7. Boswell, op. cit., 705.
8. Ibid., 705.
9. Glover, op. cit., vol. 2, 596.
10. Birmingham Public Libraries, Boulton's correspondence, 1 Dec. 1760.
11. Catalogue to the Lunar Society Exhibition, Birmingham, 1966.
12. Glover, op. cit., vol. 2, 216.
13. Hutton, W., *History of Birmingham*, VI Edition, 1835.
14. Reprinted in the *Derby Mercury*, 2 Sept. 1774.
15. Hutton, op. cit.

16. Brindley, J.M., *Churchwork in Birmingham*, 1880.
17. Colvin, op. cit., 304.
18. Gill, op. cit.

Chapter 12

1. PRO DL 42/175.
2. VCH Leics. IV, 408.
3. Davies, D.P., *A View of Derbyshire*, Derby, 1811.
4. Colvin, op. cit., 635.
5. PRO DL 41/92.
6. Joint Records Office, Lichfield, Bishop's Transcripts.
7. PRO DL 41/92.
8. Harris, J., *Sir William Chambers*, London, 1970, 229.
9. PRO DL 41/92, XC 1292 CL. Pickford to Russell, 13 May 1776.
10. Ibid.
11. Ibid.
12. PRO DL 41/92, XC 1292 CL. Pickford to Russell, 12 Feb. 1776.
13. Throsby, J., *History of Leicester*, 1791.
14. PRO DL 41/92, Agreement and Drawings, 9 March 1776.
15. PRO DL 41/92, XC 1292 CL. Richardson to Pickford, 19 Oct. 1776.
16. PRO DL 41/92, XC 1292 CL. Russell to Pickford, 22 Nov. 1776.
17. PRO DL 41/92, XC 1292 CL. King to Russell.
18. Chinnery, G.A., *Leicester Castle and the Newarke*, 1981, 12.

Chapter 13

1. The Devonshire Collections, Chatsworth House, Mr Pickford's 1st and 2nd books for the Edensor Inn, 1776–8.
2. Source unknown.
3. Broadley, A.M., *Dr Johnson and Mrs Thrale*, London, 1910, 166.
4. The Devonshire Collections, Pickford's account, 30 Nov. 1776.
5. Ibid., A map of Edensor Town, 1785.
6. Glover, S., *Peak Guide*, 1830, 56.
7. Boswell, op. cit., 881.
8. Glover, op. cit., 56.
9. The Devonshire Collections, Chatsworth and Hardwick general account book.
10. Stylistic attribution.
11. Mr M. Stanley.
12. Thompson, F., *History of Chatsworth*, 1949, 98.
13. Rhodes, E., *Peak Scenery*, 1819, vol. 2, 97–8.
14. The Devonshire Collections.
15. Ibid., Receipted account among unsorted papers.
16. Hutton, W., *History of Derby*. 1st edn. London (1791) 52–3.
17. Moritz, K.D., *Travels . . . through several parts of England* (London, 1782) 37.
18. Hutton, op. cit.

Chapter 14

1. Glover, S., op. cit., 223. The park is picturesque and landscaped; could it be the work of Emes?
2. Lysons, S. and D., *Magna Britannia*, London, 1816, vol. 5, *Derbyshire*, 31.
3. Devonshire Collections, unsorted correspondence.
4. Sheffield City Archives, Bar. D. 721.
5. Colvin, loc. cit., 47.
6. Nicolson, loc. cit., vol. 1, 237.
7. Colvin, loc. cit., 733.
8. Devonshire Collections, Chatsworth; unsorted MS account.
9. Colvin, loc. cit., 957.
10. Account book in the possession of the Every family.
11. *Derby Mercury*, 21 Aug. 1782.
12. Private collection, illustrated in Egerton, op. cit.
13. Joint Records Office, Lichfield, Bishop's Transcripts.
14. Kedleston archives, info. L. Harris.
15. Egerton, op. cit., 281–2.
16. Devonshire Collections, loc. cit., Pickford's account book.
17. *Derby Mercury*.
18. Ibid., 26 Nov. 1807.
19. Bailey's Directory.
20. Colvin, loc. cit., 555.
21. Ibid.
22. Derbys. CRO Strutt Collection.

Catalogue of Works

The authenticated works and attributions are listed together in date order. This list includes works where Pickford was the architect and where he was working as a builder to other architects' designs. A second list records proposals and other works not carried out.

FOREMARK HALL, DERBYS., for Sir Robert Burdett, supervised the building works on behalf of the architects David and William Hiorne of Warwick, 1759–61 (Burdett archives, CRO Trowbridge). At the same time work was also carried out at KNOWLE HILL, an ornamental retreat for Sir Robert Burdett; INGLEBY TOFT, a house for Robert Greaves, Burdett's agent, was built nearby.

LONGFORD HALL, DERBYS., remodelling of an Elizabethan manor-house for Wenman Coke, 1762 (Keele University, Sneyd Papers, letter from Pickford to Ralph Sneyd, 13 May 1762).

DERBY, THE ASSEMBLY ROOMS, built under Pickford's supervision 1762–5, probably to designs by Washington Shirley, 5th Earl Ferrers; interior completed by Robert Adam 1774; damaged by fire 1963; demolished 1971; façade re-erected at the Crich Tramway Museum (Derbyshire Record Office, account book signed by Pickford among the Strutt papers).

Attributed: ASHBOURNE, THE GREY HOUSE, refronted and remodelled for Brian Hodgson, 1763 (stylistic attribution); according to the Assembly Rooms' account book Pickford was working in Ashbourne in March 1763 and it is known that Hodgson was a subscriber to and served meals at the Assembly Rooms from the adjacent purpose-built supper rooms.

Attributed: ASHBOURNE, THE MANSION, refronted and remodelled for Dr John Taylor, *c.* 1764–5 (stylistic attribution); the remodelling of the interior consisted of an octagon room facing the garden which was in place by 1765 (Dr Samuel Johnson's correspondence).

Attributed: DERBY, QUEEN STREET, house remodelled for John Whitehurst, 1764 (stylistic attribution); this house was mostly demolished in 1926 after the ground floor had been converted into a shop, but photographs show Venetian and Diocletian windows in the upper storeys similar to other work by Pickford.

Attributed: DERBY, 11 FULL STREET, formerly All Saints' churchyard; house for Peter Perez Burdett in the Gothick style, built by 1765, demolished 1933. This attribution is based on Pickford's known friendship with Whitehurst, Wright and Burdett, the sophisticated style of the design, and the instructive sums of money borrowed by Burdett from Wright and Lord Ferrers (and not repaid).

Attributed: TISSINGTON HALL, ASHBOURNE, DERBYS., additional three-storey wing for William FitzHerbert, *c.* 1765 (stylistic attribution).

Attributed: ASHBOURNE, COMPTON HOUSE, for Francis Beresford, *c.* 1766 (stylistic attribution); a release of land in the Compton was made to Beresford in 1765 (deeds held by Lloyd's Bank) suggesting that the house was built shortly afterwards. The front elevation is an earlier version of No. 44 Friar Gate, Derby. The house was vacated by the Beresford family in 1840 when it became a branch of the Burton Old Bank. It is now a branch of Lloyd's.

DERBY, ST HELEN'S HOUSE, for John Gisborne, 1766–7; Pickford's claim as architect confirmed by Gianantonio Selva in 1782 (Diary in the Biblioteca Querini Stampalia, Venice); see also 'Gianantonio Selva in England', by Pierre DuPrey, *Architectural History*, vol. 25: 1982. The gate piers now at Park Road, Spondon were probably part of the screen that formerly stood in front of St Helen's House, which was removed when King Street was widened in the 1870s (information from M. Craven).

OGSTON HALL, DERBYS., design for remodelling house for William Turbutt, 1767, executed with modification by E. Stanley of Chesterfield 1768–9; altered *c.* 1840–50 and remodelled 1864 (drawings in the Derbyshire RO).

ETRURIA HALL, NR. BURSLEM, STAFFS., for Josiah Wedgwood, 1767–9 (Wedgwood's correspondence and accounts, Wedgwood Museum, Barlaston).

BANK HOUSE, ETRURIA, NR. BURSLEM, STAFFS., for Thomas Bentley, Wedgwood's partner, 1767–9; demolished 1819 (Wedgwood's correspondence and accounts, Wedgwood Museum, Barlaston).

ETRURIA WORKS, NR. BURSLEM, STAFFS., for Josiah Wedgwood, 1767–70 (Wedgwood's correspondence and accounts, Wedgwood Museum, Barlaston).

LONDON SHOWROOM, GREAT NEWPORT STREET, to display Wedgwood's wares, opened August 1768. A letter from Wedgwood to his London agent William Cox, 30 April 1968 (Wedgwood Museum, Barlaston), states that Pickford was to call on Cox and advise him on 'fitting up' the new showroom.

HAMS HALL, NR. COLESHILL, WARWICKS., work for C.B. Adderley, 1768. A letter from Josiah Wedgwood to Bentley, 15 September 1768 (Wedgwood Museum, Barlaston), mentions Pickford's employment at Hams. He may have designed this house which according to Neale's *Seats* iii, 1820, was built in 1760, and according to Burke, *Visitation of Seats* ii, 1853, 67, in 1764. It was reconstructed internally after a fire in 1890 and demolished *c.* 1920, when the upper part of the façade was rebuilt at Coates, Glos., as part of what is now Bledisloe Lodge (Colvin, *Biographical Dictionary*, 1978).

Attributed: DERBY, 35 CORNMARKET, house said to have been Heath's Bank prior to a move to Full Street in the 1770s, later associated with Charnel Bateman, attorney and member of the Derby Corporation, built *c.* 1768 (stylistic attribution).

Attributed: SHARDLOW HALL, DERBYS., wings to late seventeenth-century house for

Leonard Fosbrook *c.* 1768 (stylistic attribution). In design these wings are almost identical to those on Wanlip Hall.

DOVERIDGE HALL, DERBYS., designed by Edward Stevens for Sir Henry Cavendish, Bart., begun in 1769 (Colvin, *Biographical Dictionary* 1978). On 1 October 1770 Thomas Mottershaw wrote from Derby to Josiah Wedgwood to say that he had not seen Pickford as he had been obliged 'to return home by Ashborn therefore cou'd not call at Doveridge' (Wedgwood Museum, Barlaston). This suggests that Pickford was working there as the builder.

CALKE ABBEY, DERBYS., RIDING SCHOOL, for Sir Henry Harpur 1767–8, for the sum of £391 12s. 8d. (Harpur Crewe Archives, D2375M 184/4, Derbyshire RO).

DERBY, FRIAR GATE, Nos. 41, 44, and 45, were all plots that Pickford purchased in 1768.

> No. 41, Pickford's own house, now the Pickford House Museum, built by 1770 (T. Mozley, *Reminiscences*, 1882, and deeds in Derby Museum).
> No. 44, plot conveyed by Pickford to John Ward, silk throwster, 17 June 1769, house built by 1771 (deeds courtesy of J. Thorpe). The design for No. 44 is almost identical to the Beresford House in Ashbourne built a few years earlier.
> No. 45 conveyed to Daniel Lowe, hozier, 18 January 1771; built as a silk or wool warehouse or mill with mews, contrary to the conditions of sale. Sold to John Ward of No. 44 Friar Gate, 23 June 1778, whose heirs converted it into a house in 1799. Porch added by H.I. Stevens, architect, or his partner, who purchased the property 12 April 1872 (deeds courtesy of J. Thorpe).

In addition to the above Pickford also purchased the plot to No. 27 Friar Gate, but it would appear that he sold the plot on without being involved in the building erected in 1778 (deeds in private collection).

SANDON HALL, STAFFS., for Lord Archibald Hamilton, 1769–71; destroyed by fire 1848 (*Vitruvius Britannicus* vol. V, pp. 90–3, and archives at Sandon).

NOTTINGHAM, ST MARY'S CHURCH, design for restoration of Gothic windows, 1770 (Nottingham University Library, MAB 115).

NOTTINGHAM, THE COUNTY HALL, built by Pickford to the designs of James Gandon, 1770–2 (*Nottinghamshire County Records of the Eighteenth Century*, ed. K.T. Meaby, 1947, 54).

Attributed: SWANWICK HALL, NR. ALFRETON, DERBYS., for Hugh, the brother of the Revd John Wood, the vicar of Edensor, *c.* 1771 (stylistic attribution). As on most of Pickford's houses the architectural detail is carved out of rough rock from Horsley Castle Quarry. The building, much altered internally, is now a County Council School.

MELBOURNE HALL, DERBYS., works for Peniston Lamb, 1st Viscount Melbourne. On 17 October 1770, Melbourne wrote to his agent, Fox, 'Mr Pickford has not yet made out the plan of the room at Melbourne, but I am to see it very soon, so as to begin it early in the Spring.' It seems this work was not carried out, but in 1772 Pickford re-roofed the Hall and painted the whole building throughout for the sum of £633 6s. 9d. (Melbourne archives).

DERBY, THE SHIRE HALL, Pickford's design for the grand jury room attached to the Shire Hall, built 1659–60 by G. Eaton, was approved by Francis Noel Clarke Mundy as High Sheriff in 1772, see *Derby Mercury* advertisement, 3 July 1772, recording that Mr Pickford's plans were approved by Mundy and the Justices of the Peace on 30 June 1772. Pickford's Grand Jury Room was stripped out by Matthew Habershon in 1828 who rebuilt two courts within the shell.

WIRKSWORTH, DERBYS., THE MOOT HALL, for the Duchy of Lancaster, 1772–3; demolished and rebuilt on new site in 1814. Pickford's original design drawings are in the Public Record Office (Duchy of Lancaster archive, PRO).

Attributed: WIRKSWORTH, DERBYS., extension to house in the Market Place for John Goodwin, the solicitor who acted for the Duchy at Moot Hall, *c.* 1772. Stylistic attribution based on the fine quality of the stone window surrounds which have been largely destroyed by a recent insensitive restoration.

Attributed: BRADLEY HALL, DERBYS., conversion of large hunting stables into a house for Hugo Meynell, *c.* 1772 (stylistic attribution). The Meynell's were closely related to the FitzHerberts of Tissington and other Ashbourne families.

BIRMINGHAM, ST MARY'S CHURCH, 1773–4, on an octagonal plan with tower; demolished 1925. (Notes taken by the Revd Basil Clarke from the original Building Committee's minute book now lost. These notes are now in the Birmingham Central Library.)

CHATSWORTH, DERBYS., reconstructed the weir in the park for the 5th Duke of Devonshire in 1774. Pickford was paid £34 13s. 5d. for supervising the mason and making the drawings, that is, a guinea a day for himself and his horse and £6 6s. for his drawings and expenses at the Edensor Inn (Chatsworth archives).

CHATSWORTH, DERBYS., THE EDENSOR INN, for the 5th Duke of Devonshire, 1776–7: designed and built by Pickford for the sum of £2,551 16s. 3d. (Chatsworth archives).

CHATSWORTH, DERBYS., THE EDENSOR VICARAGE, for the Revd John Wood 1777–9. An account for 'Mr Wood's House' reads 'By sundry bills paid to Mr Pickford and others at Chatsworth 1778–9, £2360' (Chatsworth archives). Demolished 1838.

DERBY, THE DEVONSHIRE HOSPITAL, FULL STREET, for the 5th Duke of Devonshire 1777, to replace the original building founded by Bess of Hardwick in the sixteenth century. There are no building accounts, but in 1777 Pickford was paid to rehouse the inmates during the rebuilding period (Chatsworth archives). Demolished 1894.

Attributed: CHATSWORTH, DERBYS., THE LODGE GATE HOUSE, BASLOW ROAD, for the 5th Duke of Devonshire 1779 (stylistic attribution). The same craftsmen who worked on the Edensor Inn and Vicarage were also employed on this site (Chatsworth archives).

COVENTRY, HOLY TRINITY CHURCH, rebuilt three windows at the east end, 1774, and all the windows on the south side, 1775 (T. Sharp, *Illustrative Papers on the History and Antiquities of Coventry*, 1871, 107n. and Coventry RO DR 581/66, DR 801/15).

SOLIHULL CHURCH, WARWICKS., rebuilt spire 1774–5 (E.C. Sheppard, *The Tower and Bells of Solihull Church*, 1950, 20 and parish accounts, Warwicks. CRO CR 84/285 0443; DR 801/15).

TRENTHAM HALL, STAFFS., lodges for the 2nd Earl Gower, 1774–6 (drawings in the Staffs. RO).

DARLEY ABBEY, DERBYS., alterations and extensions for Robert Holden 1775–8; demolished 1962 (drawings in the Derbys. CRO).

LEICESTER, TRINITY HOSPITAL, reconstructed 1776 for the Duchy of Lancaster (the drawings and correspondence are in the Duchy papers at the PRO). The medieval chapel still stands though Pickford's work was demolished in 1898 for road widening.

Attributed: MARKEATON HALL, DERBYS., THE ORANGERY AND STABLES. Markeaton Hall was a dignified, but unspectacular redbrick mansion built on the outskirts of Derby by Wrightson Mundy, 1755. The orangery and attached quadrangle of outbuildings which we attribute to Pickford on stylistic grounds was built *c.* 1775–6 as part of the development of the park which was being laid out at this time and is attributed to William Emes. After the failure of the male line early this century, Mrs Mundy left the house and park to the Derby Corporation who demolished the house in 1964. The orangery is now used partially as a tea-room; the stables have been demolished.

Attributed: ASHFORD HALL, ASHFORD IN THE WATER, DERBYS., for John Barker, agent to the Duke of Rutland, *c.* 1776 (stylistic attribution). Letters at Chatsworth show that in the late 1770s the house was leased to Alexander Barker, agent to the Duke of Devonshire, and a kinsman of John Barker. After Barker's death in 1795 the estate passed to his son Thomas, and after his death in 1816 it was purchased by the Duke of Devonshire. The house was remodelled internally in the nineteenth century when the ground-floor windows were enlarged.

KEDLESTON HALL, DERBYS. From 1775 until his death in 1782 Pickford was employed by Lord Scarsdale to supervise the building works at Kedleston. In this capacity he succeeded James Denstone, a Derby builder, who in turn had taken over from Samuel Wyatt. It is not clear from the account books, which show only bare yearly payments, exactly what Pickford was doing there. By 1775 the last of the larger works, the bridge and the boat-house, had been completed under Denston's direction. Adam had departed, and the little design work that was left seems to have fallen to George Richardson, Adam's former assistant.

Agreements between Lord Scarsdale and Pickford survive which show that in 1775 and 1776 work was still being done in the Great Hall. Here Pickford was supervising the mason Francis Battersby who was fluting the alabaster columns (agreement dated 25 September 1775 for £180 plus £50 17s. 5d. for veneering the joints, paid 26 December 1776). At the same time George Moneypenny was doing the more intricate wood-carving to the doors and picture frames (£258 7s. 10d paid 19 October 1776). In addition Pickford supplied a chimney-piece which he valued at £80 to £85 (letter from Pickford dated 9 August 1775).

Apart from this work another building project which Pickford almost certainly undertook was the garden temple built about 1775 to the designs of George Richardson. The relationship between the two architects appears to have been cordial as Pickford subscribed to Richardson's work, *A Book of Ceilings Composed in the Style of the Antique Grotesque*, published in 1776 and dedicated to Lord Scarsdale.

Payments to Pickford taken from the Kedleston accounts:

1776	Pickford on account of the buildings	£1,000		
1777	Pickford balance of his a/c up to January 1777	£	861	9s. 0d.
1777	Pickford £	49 19s. 6d.		
1778	Pickford £	313 19s. 8d.		
1779	Pickford £	40 11s. 6d.		
1781	Pickford up to 21 February 1781	£	79	1s. 9d.
1781	Pickford £	50 1s 5d.		
1783	Pickford £	185 5s. 6d.		
1785	Basset (by order Mr Pickford and Mr Seal)	£	32	4s. 4d.

The payments made after Pickford's death in July 1782 were probably a settlement for work done by subcontractors while he was living. (For the above information from the Kedleston archives we are indebted to Mr Leslie Harris.)

Attributed: WANLIP HALL, LEICS., for Sir Charles Grave Hudson (stylistic attribution). According to Nichols (*Leicestershire*, vol. 3) the old house was demolished in 1768 and the new one completed by 1778. Nichols also tells us that Hudson was a FRS, which suggests that he was acquainted with John Whitehurst and his circle of midland intellectuals.

LONG EATON HALL, DERBYS., built for John Howitt *c.* 1778, now the offices of the Erewash DC (stylistic attribution). The front door surround is carved out of rough rock from Horsley Castle Quarry. Inside, fine timber staircase and marble fireplace are attributed to George Moneypenny.

DRAYCOTT HOUSE, DERBYS., built for William Evans of Derby *c.* 1781 (stylistic attribution). The house is similar in style and proportion to Long Eaton Hall built a few years earlier.

Proposals and Works Not Carried Out

BIRMINGHAM, SOHO, proposals for a new house for Matthew Boulton. In a letter to Boulton dated 1 December 1760 (Boulton papers, Birmingham Central Library), Pickford stated that he would 'take care to get you sketches made for your new house very soon';. The name of the architect of Soho Hall is not known, but Timothy Lightoler commenced building the Soho Works in 1761. He was superseded by Benj. Wyatt & Co. about 1765 who also completed the house which was begun a few years earlier (Colvin's *Dictionary of British Architects*, pp. 520 and 936).

KEELE HALL, STAFFS., proposals to Ralph Sneyd, dated 1 August 1761, to rebuild part of the house and for new offices, not carried out (Sneyd archive, Keele University).

CALKE ABBEY, DERBYS., proposals for a new house for Sir Henry Harpur *c.* 1764, not carried out. The unsigned and probably unsolicitored drawings were found at Calke Abbey by Howard Colvin and are now deposited at the Derbys. RO. The drawings are attributed to Pickford on style of draughtsmanship.

BROCKET HALL, HERTS., a payment to Pickford of £20, 'for the drawings for Brockett' is recorded in Viscount Melbourne's accounts in 1772 (Melbourne archives). At this date Brocket Hall was being rebuilt by James Paine and at present it is not known what the payment was for.

Select Bibliography

Adam, Robert E. James, *Works in Architecture*, 1773.

Bemrose, W., *The Life and Works of Joseph Wright*, Derby, 1855.

Boswell, J., *Life of Samuel Johnson, The World's Classics*, Oxford University Press, 1360–1.

Broadley, A.M., *Dr Johnson and Mrs Thrale*, London, 1910.

Byng, Hon. J., *The Torrington Diaries* (ed. C. Andrews), London, 1935.

Chinnery, G.A., *Leicester Castle and the Newarke*, 1981.

Colvin, H.M. *Biographical Dictionary of British Architects 1660–1840*, London, 1978.

— (ed.), *History of the King's Works*, vol. V.

Christian, R., *The Butterley Company*, London, 1990.

Craven, M., *The Derby Town House*, Derby, 1978.

—, *The Derbyshire Country House*, Derby, 1991.

Darwin, E., *The Economy of Vegitation*, 1791.

Davies, D.P., *A View of Derbyshire*, Derby, 1811.

DNB, Combined Edition, 2 vols., Oxford, 1975.

Defoe, D., *A Tour Through the Whole Island of Great Britain* (ed. P. Rogers), London, 1986.

Gandon, J., *Vitruvius Britannicus*, vol. V, London, 1771.

Glover, S., *A History and Gazetteer of the County of Derby*, Derby, 1829–31.

—, *Peak Guide*, 1830.

Gunnis, R., *Dictionary of British Sculptors, 1660–1851*, London, 1953.

Harris, J., *Sir William Chambers*, London, 1970.

Hutton, W., *The History of Derby*, London, 1791.

—, *History of Birmingham*, VI Edition, 1835.

King-Hele, D., *Doctor of Revolution*, London, 1977.

—, *The Letters of Erasmus Darwin*, Cambridge University Press, 1981.

Lysons, S. and D., *Magna Britannia*, London, 1816.

Meaby, K.T. (ed.), *Nottingham County Records of the Eighteenth Century*, 1947.

Meteyard, E., *The Life of Josiah Wedgwood*, 2 vols., 1865.

Mozley, T., *Reminiscences*, 1882.

Nicolson, B., *Joseph Wright of Derby*, London, 1968.
Pevsner, Sir N., *Derbyshire*, London, 1953.
Phillips, Sir R., *A Personal Tour through the U.K.*, London, 1828.
Rhodes, E., *Peak Scenery*, 1819.
Seward, A., *Memoirs of the Life of Dr Johnson*, 1804.
Thompson, F., *History of Chatsworth*, 1949.
Throsby, J., *Select Views of Leicestershire . . .*, Leicester, 1789.
—, *History of Leicester*, 1791.
Vardy, J., *Some Designs of Mr Inigo Jones and Mr William Kent*, 1744.
Wedgwood, B. and H., *The Wedgwood Circle, 1730–1897*, 1980.
Willis, R. and Clarke, J., *The Architectural History of the University of Cambridge*, 3 vols.
Wittkower, R., *Palladio and English Palladianism*, London, 1947.

Picture Credits

The author and publishers are grateful to the following for their permission to reproduce photographs in this book: H.M. Colvin, pp. 6, 12; M. Craven, pp. 4, 31, 47, 52, 74, 85, 88, 95, 104, 105, 108, 116, 134, 141, 143, 150, 153; Derby Museum, pp. 19, 26, 27, 28, 30, 34, 35, 60, 63, 65, 66, 86, 91, 96, 99, 103, 106, 107, 145, 155b; Derbyshire CRO, pp. 36, 61, 126, 127, 128; National Trust, p. 54; I. Shaw, pp. 17, 48, 55, 58, 70, 72, 80, 84, 136, 137, 138, 139, 147, 148, 149, 154; Staffordshire CRO, pp. 112, 114, 115. The photographs on pp. 21, 22 and 25 are from private collections. All remaining photographs are from the author.

Index

Hodgson, Brian (1706–84), 69–71, 80, 153, 169
Holdon family, 34–5
Holden, Robert (d. 1780), 173
Holkham Hall, Norf., 12, 13, 115
Holland, Henry (1745–1806), 115, 116
Hope, Revd Charles (1732–98), 29
Hopton Wood stone, 76, 81, 86, 106
Horse Guards, see London
Horsley Castle Quarry, 142, 171, 174
Horton family, 87
Houghton, Norf., 55, 56
Howdalian Society, 23, 33
Howdall, Capt., R.A., 23, 33
Howitt, John, 174
Hudson, Sir Charles Grave, 1st Bt., of Wanlip (1730–1813), 117
Hudson, Thomas (1701–79), 23
Hull, Yorks., Maister's House, 85
Hume, David (1711–76), 68
Humphrey, Ozias, 24
Hurt, Francis (d. 1801), 157
Hutton, William (1723–1815), 86, 122, 144
Hyde, Lord see Villiers
Hyde Park Corner, see London

Ince Blundell Hall, Lancs., 76
Ingleby Toft, Derbys., 50, 169
Italy, 24, 55, 150
Ivory, Thomas (1709–79), 119

Jelf, Andrews (d. 1759), 12, 15
Johnson, Dr Samuel (1709–84), 68, 71–4, 75, 79, 121, 135, 140
Jones, Inigo (1573–1652), 40, 53, 57, 84
Judd, Thomas, 10

Kedleston Hall, Derbys., 32, 50, 66, 86, 135, 158, 173–4
Keele Hall, Staffs., 41–2, 51–3, 71, 174
Keir, Capt. James (1735–1820), 27, 94
Kent, William (d. 1748), 12, 84, 115, 148
King, Mr, 133
Kirk Langley, Derbys., 101
Knightley, Miss, 102
Knowle Hill, Derbys., 29, 48, 50, 169
Kyre Park, Worcs., 71

Lamb, Sir Matthew (d. 1768), 116
Lamb, Sir Peniston, 1st Viscount Melbourne (1748–1828), 116, 171, 174
Lancaster, Duchy of, 38, 125, 131–4, 172–3
Langley, Batty (1696–1751), 76
Lansdowne, Lord, see FitzMaurice
Lea, Anne, 7
Leicester, 117, 159
  County Gaol, 159
  Earls of, see Coke
  Infirmary, 117
  Newarke, 131
  Trinity Hospital, 125, 130–4, 173
Leigh, Edward, 3rd Lord (d. 1738), 8

Leveson-Gower, see Gower
Ley, Thomas (d. 1795), 154
Lichfield, Staffs., 10, 22, 68, 79, 90, 92
  Botanical Society, 68
Lightoler, Timothy, 51, 174
Liverpool, Lancs., 22, 29, 76
Loaden Hall, Seighford, Staffs., 105
London, 3, 7, 10, 11–16, 23, 27, 33, 40, 53, 55, 78, 82, 97, 158
  Finch House, Berkeley Sq., 12
  Fleet St, 27
  Gower House, 115
  Great Newport St, 11, 97–8, 170
  Green Park, 11
  Horse Guards, 12, 15, 83
  Hyde Park Corner, 14–15, 17
  Lansdowne House, 77, 84, 140
  Mayfair, 11
  Pelham House, Arlington St, 12–13
  Picadilly, 11
  St Bride, Fleet St, 11
  Savoy chapel, 128
  Westminster Hall, 40
Long Eaton Hall, Derbys., 174
Longford Hall, Derbys., 18–19, 51–2, 169
Lowe, Daniel (1739–98), 109, 171
Lunar Society, 20, 24, 27–8, 83, 84, 90, 94, 121
Lysons, Samuel & Daniel, 146

Mackworth, Derbys., 101
Manners, Dukes of Rutland, 146, 147, 173
Markeaton Brook, Derbys., 110
  Hall, 67, 101, 173
  Orangery at, 173
Marylebone, Mx., 78
Mason, Revd William (1724–97), 30
Masons', Worshipful Company of, 11
Mayfair, see London
Mayfield, Staffs., 154–6
Melbourne, Derbys., 8
  Hall, 116, 171
  Lord, see Lamb
Melton, Philip, 140
Meteyard, Eliza, 94
Meynell family, of Bradley, Derbys., 68, 78–9, 172
Meynell, Hugo (1735–1808), 78–9, 172
Meynell, Littleton Poyntz (d. 1753), 79
Meynell, Mary, 79
Moneypenny, Anne, 156, 158
Moneypenny, George, the elder (d. 1807), 71, 122, 128–9, 140, 147–59, 173–4
Moneypenny, George, the younger, 158–9
Montigny, Jean, 11
Morteboys, Mary, 5, 7
Mortimer, John Hamilton (1741–79), 23
Mottershaw, Thomas, 24, 171
Mozley, Revd Thomas (1806–93), 20, 36, 38, 102, 171
Munday's Coffee House, 23
Mundy, Emily Georgiana (d. 1929), 173
Mundy family, 67, 173